Microwave Menus

D1514468

HOME COOKING

© 1994 Time-Life Books B.V.
First published jointly by Time-Life Books B.V. and
Geddes & Grosset Ltd.

Material in this book was first published as part of the series
HEALTHY HOME COOKING.

All rights reserved.
No part of this book may be reproduced in any form or by any
electronic or mechanical means, including information storage
and retrieval devices or systems, without prior written permission
from the publisher.

ISBN 0 7054 2039 6

Printed in EC.

Microwave Menus

BY

THE EDITORS OF TIME-LIFE BOOKS

TIME-LIFE/GEDDES & GROSSET

Contents

The Miracle of the Microwave

The microwave oven is an invaluable ally to the busy cook seeking first-rate results. Vegetables display hidden depths of subtly and flavour. Fish and shellfish retain a delicacy and juiciness often lost when treated in orthodox ways. Fresh herbs do not fade or blacken. Spices such as yellow mustard seeds remain bright and vibrant.

Things happen faster in a microwave, and many of these recipes are cooked in moments. In the creation of hors-d'oeurves this is an attractive factor; but for a cook in the throws of dinner party preparation, the most alluring of the microwave's advantages may be its efficiency. With the first course underway in the microwave, the stove is completely free for the rest of the menu.

A microwave is the ideal vehicle for quick soups and stews, as the recipe for broccoli soup (page 17), shows. Because microwaving is so quick, flavour may not mingle and meld as they do when soups and stews are cooked conventionally. But there are ways around this dilemma. The seafood stew (page 19) adopts a proven stratagem: a touch of sugar brings unity to the dish. The light vegetable soup (page 16), a melange of mange-tout, courgettes, carrots and lettuce—still crisp because the cooking time is only 6 minutes—comes vividly to life through the addition of Dijon mustard.

An important aspect of microwave cookery is that few of the vitamins and minerals are lost in the cooking process, a hazard in conventional cookery which can reduce the goodness of even the most healthy dish. This is because in microwaves vegetables cook in their own juices, or with only a few spoonfuls of added liquid. Also, because cooking times are generally so short, heat-sensitive vitamins are less likely to be destroyed by microwaving than by traditional techniques. Microwave ovens are ideal for low-fat cookery too; very little oil is required for the preparation of most vegetable dishes.

The vegetarian recipes suggest the enticing array of meatless meals that can be produced from a microwave oven. The microwave even allows the cook to add a surprising twist to familiar stand-bys, such as in the salad filled potato pie (page 22). Several of the recipes are inspired by the far-flung traditional cuisines not usually associated with this space-age technology. The Oriental parchment parcels (page 24) retains its original delicate, sophisticated taste. The egg batter of the Clafoutis (page 21) offers a tender base of the Gallic combination of baked cherry tomatoes and courgettes.

To some, microwaving may seem like an inappropriate way to cook pasta. But the fact is that pasta can be microwaved in relatively little water—or without any water at all when sauce or stock is substituted.

The trick is to provide just enough moisture for the pasta to absorb. The moisture renders it subtle and produces the desired al dente quality of the boiled product. But the cook must still check for doneness to avoid the pasta turning soft and sticky, and note that the food will continue cooking for several minutes after it has been removed from the oven.

Freshness of flavour, high nutritional value, speedy preparation— these beneficent basics of fish and shellfish cookery get an extra boost from the microwave oven. Fish steaks and fillets are the best candidates for microwaving; their uniform texture and shape allow them to cook evenly. For best results, place the thicker portions towards the outside of the dish or overlap the thinner sections in wreathlike fashion. Then cover the dish with plastic film and set the oven on high power. The result are similar to conventional steaming or poaching.

Shellfish also cook to advantage in a microwave oven. Prawns, scallops, oysters and clams need only 2 to 3 minutes per 500 g (1 lb); however, they should be stirred half way through the process.

Poultry can also be cooked with a minimum of fuss. A whole, unstuffed 1.5 kg (3 lb) chicken, for example, requires only about 20 minutes roasting time, plus another 7 minutes standing time during which the meat continues to cook. Chicken joints need only 6 to 7 minutes cooking per 500 g (1 lb)—about one quarter the usual time.

Microwave cooking will also render more fat from chicken or turkey than conventional methods do. And as mentioned earlier, fewer of the nutrients will be lost.

Most microwaves are ineffective in browning foods since the air within the oven does not heat up in the same way as the food does and thus cannot effect the foods surface. Taking this drawback into account, *Home Cooking* have created six microwave poultry dishes which please the eye as much as the palate by including colourful vegetables and appropriate sauces. The tarragon-cream sauce *(page 40)* is an excellent example of how the microwave can retain the sharp colours of herbs and spices, making up for its lack of browning ability.

The pork recipes in this book are chosen to show how some dishes are actually improved by cooking in the microwave oven. Because the process of mincing breaks down the meats's fibres, minced pork is particularly suited to rapid cooking in the microwave oven. Chops also benefit from microwave cooking. When chops are fried or grilled, the time required for the meat round the bone to cook through properly can cause the outside to become dried out and tough; in the microwave the chops will cook through evenly, so that the inside will be ready at the time as the outside.

The speed of microwave cookery is most evident in the case of stews and casserole dishes. The recipe for pork in cider *(page 44)*, cooks in just 15 minutes in the microwave oven, plus 5 minutes for thickening the liquid, and all the other casserole recipes are cooked in under an hour. The microwave oven also provides the quickest means of preparing the constituent ingredients—such as the winter squash in the golden casserole *(page 45.)*

Several of the recipes call for the use of a browning dish, a glass-ceramic grill or dish with a tin-oxide coating that colours the meat in the same way as the initial searing at high temperatures in conventional cooking. Always follow the manufacturer's instructions strictly when using the dish, as overheating can damage it. Also, when covering a microwave dish containing liquid with greaseproof paper or microwave-safe plastic film, take care to leave one corner loose to prevent a build up of steam.

A microwave oven encourages invention—and never more so perhaps, than in the case of beef, for the meat may be prepared successfully in any number of ways in a fraction of the time it would take by conventional cooking methods. Sealed in an oven-cooking bag and microwaved on medium power, for example, a roast braises on its own juices. It might also be cut into strips for a dish that looks and tastes like a stir-fry with very little oil, or stuffed with a vegetable filling and served sliced.

A few simple techniques ensure success. Cutting the beef into smaller pieces helps it cook more evenly in the microwave oven, but roasts can also be cooked whole. To keep the meat from drying out, cover the roast during cooking. Avoid salting the roast beforehand—this tends to toughen the meat and leach natural salts and moisture.

For the sake of succulence, tender cuts of beef—including escalopes and meatballs—should be microwaved on high (100 per cent power). Less tender cuts such as those from the topside of beef, should be tightly covered and then simmered in liquid on medium (50 per cent power).

The same rules apply when cooking lamb in the microwave. Adhering to the basic guidelines can produce a variety of dishes such as chilli meatballs *(page 57)* or the minced lamb loaf *(page 58)*.

A crucial element is the 'standing time'—a period after the food has been removed from the oven but continues to cook. This can account for up to half the total cooking time. Test for doneness only at the end of standing time. With a roast, testing is simplified by using a meat thermometer inserted into the thickest part.

Lastly, puddings, custards and fruits may seem unlikely candidates for the microwave oven, but they are only a few of the many desserts which are suited to the microwave process. When prepared conventionally, some puddings and custards require constant stirring to keep the mixture smooth and prevent it from burning. In the microwave they need only be stirred occasionally, and there is no danger of scorching them.

Because of their high juice content, fruits that are baked in the microwave require little added liquid—and, since they cook quickly, they lose few of their water-soluble vitamins. Fruits retain their shape, texture and much of their inviting colour as well. One caution: avoid microwaving overripe fruits—they may soften to the point of disintegration.

Since some cakes fail to brown in the microwave, they are not suitable for the process. Still, cakes that have colour in themselves, such as those made with chocolate, or those with fruit in the bottom, fare very well indeed, as proven by the chocolate pudding cake *(page 59)* and the rhubarb-gingerbread upside-down cake *(page 60)*.

The simple chore associated with dessert preparation can be abbreviated. Not only does the microwave dispense with the double boiler used for melting chocolate, but it can melt 30 g (1 oz) of chocolate in just $1^1/_2$ to 2 minutes—less than one third the customary time.

Although power settings often vary among different manufacturers' ovens, the recipes use 'high' to indicate 100 per cent power, 'medium high' for 70 per cent power, 'medium' for 50 per cent and 'medium low' for 30 per cent. All custards, puddings and fruits are microwaved on high.

The Key to Better Eating

Home Cooking addresses the concerns of today's weight-conscious, health-minded cooks with recipes that take into account guidelines set by nutritionists. The secret of eating well, of course, has to do with maintaining a balance of foods in the diet. The recipes thus should be used thoughtfully, in the context of a day's eating. To make the choice easier, an analysis is given of nutrients in a single serving. The counts for calories, protein, cholesterol, total fat, saturated fat and sodium are approximate.

Interpreting the chart

The chart below gives dietary guidelines for healthy men, women and children. Recommended figures vary from country to country, but the principles are the same everywhere. Here, the average daily amounts of calories and protein are from a report by the UK Department of Health and Social Security; the maximum advisable daily intake of fat is based on guidelines given by the National Advisory Committee on Nutrition Education (NACNE); those for cholesterol and sodium are based on upper limits suggested by the World Health Organization.

The volumes in the Home Cooking series do not purport to be diet books, nor do they focus on health foods. Rather, they express a common-sense approach to cooking that uses salt, sugar, cream, butter and oil in moderation while employing other ingredients that also provide flavour and satisfaction. The portions themselves are modest in size.

The recipes make few unusual demands. Naturally they call for fresh ingredients, offering substitutes when these are unavailable. (The substitute is not calculated in the nutrient analysis, however.) Most of the ingredients can be found in any well-stocked supermarket.

Heavy-bottomed pots and pans are recommended to guard against burning whenever a small amount of oil is used and where there is danger of the food adhering to the hot surface, but non-stick pans can be utilized as well. Both safflower oil and virgin olive oil are favoured for sautéing. Safflower oil was chosen because it is the most highly polyunsaturated vegetable fat available in supermarkets, and polyunsaturated fats reduce blood cholesterol; if unobtainable, use sunflower oil, also high in polyunsaturated fats. Virgin olive oil is used because it has a fine fruity flavour lacking in the lesser grade known as 'pure'. In addition, it is—like all olive oil—high in mono-unsaturated fats, which are thought not to increase blood cholesterol. When virgin olive oil is unavailable, or when its flavour is not essential to the success of the dish, 'pure' may be used.

About cooking times

To help planning, time is taken into account in the recipes. While recognizing that everyone cooks at a different speed and that stoves and ovens differ, approximate 'working' and 'total' times are provided. Working time stands for the minutes actively spent on preparation; total time includes unattended cooking time, as well as time devoted to marinating, steeping or soaking ingredients. Since the recipes emphasize fresh foods, they may take a bit longer to prepare than 'quick and easy' dishes that call for canned or packaged products, but the difference in flavour, and often in nutrition, should compensate for the little extra time involved.

Recommended Dietary Guidelines

Average Daily Intake			Maximum Daily Intake				
		Calories	Protein grams	Cholesterol milligrams	Total fat grams	Saturated fat grams	Sodium milligrams
Females	7-8	1900	47	300	80	32	2000*
	9-11	2050	51	300	77	35	2000
	12-17	2150	53	300	81	36	2000
	18-54	2150	54	300	81	36	2000
	55-74	1900	47	300	72	32	2000
Males	7-8	1980	49	300	80	33	2000
	9-11	2280	57	300	77	38	2000
	12-14	2640	66	300	99	44	2000
	15-17	2880	72	300	108	48	2000
	18-34	2900	72	300	109	48	2000
	35-64	2750	69	300	104	35	2000
	65-74	2400	60	300	91	40	2000

* (or 5g salt)

Aubergines Stuffed with Lamb and Buckwheat

When aubergines are to be cooked by conventional methods they are often salted and rinsed first to draw out their bitter juices. Cooks have found that this step is unnecessary when aubergines are microwaved.

Serves 4

Working (and total) time: about 40 minutes

Calories 200, Protein 13g, Cholesterol 30mg, Total fat 11g, Saturated fat 2g, Sodium 140mg

30 g/1 oz	*roasted buckwheat groats (kasha)*
2	*aubergines (about 200 g/7 oz each), stalks left on, skins pierced two or three times with a skewer*
1	*small onion, finely chopped*
1 tbsp	*safflower oil*
30 g/2 oz	*pine-nuts, finely chopped*
150 g/5 oz	*leftover cooked lean ham, minced*
3 tsp	*chopped fresh oregano, or ¹/₂ tsp dried oregano*
4	*medium tomatoes, puréed in a blender, sieved, skins and seeds discarded*
1 tbsp	*chopped parsley*
	freshly ground black pepper

Place the buckwheat groats in a small bowl and microwave on high for 30 seconds. Add 12.5 cl (4 fl oz) of hot water and microwave on high until the water is nearly absorbed—about 4 minutes more. Cover the buckwheat with plastic film and set it aside.

Arrange the aubergines in a deep baking dish and add 4 tablespoons of water. Cover with plastic film, leaving a corner open. Microwave on high until they are soft and their colour fades—about 10 minutes.

Meanwhile, prepare the stuffing. Put the onion in a glass bowl with the oil and microwave on high until soft—about 3 to 4 minutes. Stir in the pine-nuts and microwave on high for 1 minute; stir again and microwave on high until the nuts begin to brown—about 30 seconds. Stir in the lamb, oregano, buckwheat, paprika, salt and 2 tablespoons of the puréed tomato.

Halve the aubergines lengthwise. With a spoon, scoop out most of the flesh from each aubergine half, leaving a shell about 5 cm (¹/₄ inch) thick. Chop the flesh, stir it into the lamb and buckwheat, and pile this stuffing into the aubergine shells. Arrange the shells on a serving platter, leaving a space in the centre for a small bowl. Cover the aubergines with non-stick parchment paper and microwave on high until hot—about 4 minutes. Sprinkle with the parsley.

Meanwhile, season the remaining puréed tomato with plenty of pepper. Put the purée in a serving bowl and microwave on high for 1 minute. Place the bowl of purée in the centre of the aubergines and serve.

EDITOR'S NOTE: This dish may also be prepared with 125 g (5 oz) very lean raw minced lamb. Crumble the lamb on to a glass plate, cover the plate with a paper towel and microwave it on high for a total of 90 seconds, stirring after 45 seconds.

Plaice with Lemon and Parsley

MICROWAVING FISH FILLETS ON A BED OF HERBS AND AROMATIC VEGETABLES RETAINS THE MOISTURE AND ENHANCES THE FLAVOUR.

Serves 8

Working (and total) time: about 30 minutes

Calories 65, Protein 11g, Cholesterol 35mg, Total fat 2g, Saturated fat 0g, Sodium 125mg

8	plaice fillets (about 125 g/4 oz each), skinned
1/8 tsp	salt
	freshly ground black pepper
1	small onion, very finely chopped
2 tbsp	finely chopped parsley
3 tbsp	fresh lemon juice
4 tbsp	white wine
8	thin lemon slices

Lay the fillets flat on a work surface, skinned side up. Season them with the salt and some pepper.

In the base of a shallow serving dish, spread out the onion and parsley, and sprinkle with the lemon juice and white wine. Double over each fillet, with the skinned side in, and arrange the fillets on top of the onion and parsley in two overlapping rows. Tuck the lemon slices between the fillets.

Cover the dish loosely with plastic film, then microwave on high until the fish is opaque—3 to 4 minutes. Rotate the dish once during the cooking time.

Let the fish stand, still covered with plastic film, for 3 minutes. Then remove the film and serve the plaice straight from the dish, spooning a little of the cooking liquid over each fillet.

EDITOR'S NOTE: The fish and its cooking liquid may also be served cold, garnished with a salad of radicchio leaves.

Stuffed Artichokes

BREADCRUMB-STUFFED ARTICHOKES OFTEN APPEAR IN SICILIAN AND
SOUTHERN ITALIAN COOKERY. ARTICHOKES NOT ONLY COOK FASTER IN
THE MICROWAVE BUT ALSO RETAIN A FRESHER, GREENER COLOUR THAN
WHEN STEAMED ON THE STOVE.

Serves 4
Working time: about 40 minutes
Total time: about 1 hour
Calories 210, Protein 10g, Cholesterol 15mg, Total fat 12g,
Saturated fat 12g, Sodium 295mg

125 g/4 oz	*fresh wholemeal breadcrumbs*
4	*artichokes*
1¹/2 tbsp	*fresh lemon juice*
4 tbsp	*finely grated Parmesan cheese*
2 tbsp	*virgin olive oil*
2	*cloves garlic, crushed*
2 tbsp	*finely chopped parsley*
	freshly ground black pepper

Spread the breadcrumbs for the stuffing in a shallow
layer on a plate and microwave, uncovered, on high
until they start to crisp—3 to 4 minutes. Set the crumbs
aside while you prepare the artichokes.

Discard the artichoke stalks, cutting them level with
the base so that the artichokes stand upright. With a
small, sharp knife, trim away about 1 cm (¹/2 inch) from
the tips of all the pointed leaves, and slice off about
2.5 cm (1 inch) from the top of each artichoke. Once
cut, artichokes quickly lose their colour when exposed
to the air; keep them green by dipping each one in
water acidulated with 1 tablespoon of the lemon juice.

To cook the artichokes, measure 30 cl (¹/2 pint) water and the remaining lemon juice into a dish that will
be large enough to hold the artichokes compactly.
Microwave the liquid, uncovered, on high until it boils—
about 4 minutes. Arrange the drained artichokes, stalk
ends up, in the hot liquid. Cover with plastic film, leav-

ing a corner open, and microwave on high for 12 minutes. Remove the dish from the microwave and turn each artichoke upside down. Cover again with plastic film and microwave until the leaves can be pulled away easily and the base of each artichoke is readily pierced with a fork—4 to 8 minutes, depending on their size.

Meanwhile, prepare the stuffing. In a small mixing bowl, combine the breadcrumbs with the cheese. Make a well in the centre and pour the oil into this hollow. With a fork, mix the crushed garlic and the parsley into the oil, grind in some black pepper and stir until all the ingredients are thoroughly blended.

Drain the cooked artichokes in a colander and stand them upright on a board. With your fingers, draw open the centre of each artichoke and pull out and discard a few of the central leaves. Using a teaspoon, scoop out and discard the hairy choke.

Gently draw the leaves away from the body of each artichoke to form pockets, and pack the openings loosely with the breadcrumb mixture. Sprinkle the remaining crumbs over the top of the artichokes.

Arrange the stuffed artichokes on a serving dish. Cover them with plastic film, leaving one corner open, and microwave on high until the artichokes are heated through—6 to 8 minutes. Serve the artichokes hot.

Tomatoes with a Spinach and Tofu Stuffing

Serves 4
Working (and total) time: about 35 minutes
Calories 150, Protein 9g, Cholesterol 5mg, Total fat 8g,
Saturated fat 2g, Sodium 280mg

1 tbsp	*flaked almonds*
350 g/12 oz	*spinach, stalks removed, leaves washed and finely shredded*
2	*beef tomatoes (about 500 g/1 lb)*
60 g/2 oz	*smoked tofu*
1 tbsp	*grated Parmesan cheese*
2 tbsp	*fresh wholemeal breadcrumbs*
2 tsp	*finely shredded fresh basil, or ¹/₂ tsp dried basil*
	freshly ground black pepper
¹/₈ tsp	*salt*
1 tbsp	*virgin olive oil*

In a heavy frying pan, toss the almonds over high heat until they are golden-brown—about 1 minute.

Put the shredded spinach leaves in a bowl, cover them loosely with plastic film or with a lid, and microwave them on high for 3 minutes. Transfer the cooked spinach to a colander to drain thoroughly. Press the leaves gently to remove as much water as possible.

While the spinach drains, halve the tomatoes horizontally, scoop out their seeds with a spoon and discard the seeds. Using a sharp knife, cut out and reserve the tomato pulp. Chop 1 tablespoon of the pulp and set it aside; reserve the rest for another use.

To prepare the stuffing, finely chop the tofu and mix it with the spinach, chopped tomato pulp, Parmesan cheese, breadcrumbs, basil and some freshly ground pepper. Season the hollowed-out tomatoes with the salt and more pepper, then press the mixture into them with a spoon. Sprinkle a little of the olive oil over the top of each tomato.

Place the stuffed tomatoes on a serving dish and microwave them, uncovered, on medium low for 5 minutes. Give each tomato a half turn, then microwave them on low until the tomato shells are tender—3 to 5 minutes more.

Garnish the top of each stuffed tomato with the toasted almond flakes and serve hot.

EDITOR'S NOTE: Stuffed beef tomatoes make a substantial starter; for a lighter hors-d'oeuvre, you can substitute a smaller variety of firm-fleshed tomato and halve the quantity of stuffing. Smoked tofu (bean curd) is available from Oriental and health food shops, if it is unobtainable, however, plain tofu may be substituted.

Bacon-Stuffed Mushrooms

Serves 4

Working (and total) time: about 20 minutes

Calories 100, Protein 7g, Cholesterol 15mg, Total fat 6g,
Saturated fat 2g, Sodium 500mg

4	*large field mushrooms (about 300g/10 oz), rinsed, dried, stalks removed*
1 tbsp	*dry vermouth*
4 tbsp	*coarsely chopped parsley*
100 g/3^1/2 oz	*lean unsmoked bacon rashers, trimmed of rind and all fat*
1	*garlic clove, crushed*
1 tbsp	*virgin olive oil*
15 g/^{1}/2 oz	*fresh wholemeal breadcrumbs*
	freshly ground black pepper

Arrange the mushroom caps upside down in a single layer in a shallow dish, and sprinkle them with the dry vermouth and parsley. Cover the mushroom caps loosely with plastic film.

To make the stuffing, cut the bacon into small strips. Put the bacon and the crushed garlic in a bowl, stir in the olive oil, and microwave on high until the bacon begins to release its juices—about 1 minute. Stir the breadcrumbs and some pepper into the bacon mixture. Microwave the mixture on high until it is crisp—about 1 minute. Cover the stuffing with plastic film and keep it warm while you cook the mushrooms.

Leaving the mushrooms loosely covered, microwave them on high for 3 minutes, until they are just tender. Remove the plastic film, spread the bacon stuffing on top of the mushroom caps, and microwave on high until they are hot—about 30 seconds. Serve the stuffed mushrooms immediately.

Baby Beetroots in Orange and Walnut Dressing

Serves 4

Working time: about 30 minutes

Total time: about 45 minutes

Calories 105, Protein 2g, Cholesterol 0mg, Total fat 9g, Saturated fat 1g, Sodium 40mg

6	*small beetroots (about 350 g/12 oz), careful scrubbed clean but unpeeled*
1 tbsp	*walnut oil*
1 tbsp	*safflower oil*
2 tbsp	*fresh orange juice*
1 tsp	*grated orange rind*
15 g/¹/₂ oz	*shelled walnuts, finely chopped*
	freshly ground black pepper
90 g/3 oz	*curly endive*
1	*onion, sliced into thin rings*

Put the beetroots into a casserole and add hot water to reach half way up the beetroots. Cover the casserole and microwave on high for 10 minutes. Using a spoon, turn the beetroots over, then replace the lid and continue microwaving until the beetroots are just tender—about 7 minutes more.

Remove the beetroots from the casserole with a slotted spoon and leave them to cool while you make the dressing. In a small bowl, beat together the walnut oil, safflower oil, orange juice, grated orange rind, chopped walnuts and some pepper.

When the beetroots are cool enough to handle, peel them with a sharp knife. Divide the curly endive among four plates. Cut the beetroots into thin rounds and arrange them, together with the onion rings, on top of the beds of curly endive leaves.

Stir the dressing rapidly with a fork and pour it over the beetroot slices and onions, making sure that the walnuts are evenly distributed.

Light Vegetable Stew with Mange-Tout and Mustard

Serves 6 as a side dish
Working (and total) time: about 25 minutes
Calories 70, Protein 2g, Cholesterol 10mg, Total fat 4g, Saturated fat 2g, Sodium 95mg

1	*courgette, halved lengthwise and cut diagonally into 5 mm (¹/₄ inch) thick slices*
1 tbsp	*fresh lemon juice*
30 g/1 oz	*unsalted butter, cut into pieces*
2	*carrots, cut diagonally into 5 mm (¹/₄ inch) thick ovals*
1	*shallot, finely chopped*
1 tbsp	*Dijon mustard*
1	*cos lettuce, cored, the leaves torn into 5 cm (2 inch) pieces*
1 tsp	*fresh thyme, or ¹/₄ tsp dried thyme*
¹/₈ tsp	*salt*
	freshly ground black pepper
125 g/4 oz	*mange-tout, any stems and strings removed, large pods halved diagonally*

Put the courgette slices into a small bowl, toss the with the lemon juice, and set the bowl aside.

Put the butter into a large bowl and microwave it on high until it melts—about 1 minute. Stir in the carrots, shallot and mustard. Cook the mixture on high for 2 minutes, stirring half way through the cooking time.

Add the lettuce, thyme, salt and some pepper; stir the vegetables to coat them with the butter. Microwave the stew on high for 1 minute, stirring once after 30 seconds. Stir in the courgette slices and lemon juice, then the mange-tout. Cook the stew on high for minutes more, stirring once half way through the cooking time. Stir the vegetables one last time, cover the bowl and let the stew stand for another 3 minute before serving it.

Broccoli Soup
with Cumin and Scallops

Serves 8

Working time: about 20 minutes

Total time: about 50 minutes

Calories 140, Protein 8g, Cholesterol 30mg, Total fat 7g,
Saturated fat 4g, Sodium 280mg

30 g/1 oz	*unsalted butter*
500 g/1 lb	*broccoli, florets cut off, stems peeled and cut into 2.5 cm (1 inch) lengths*
2	*leeks, split, washed thoroughly to remove all grit, and thinly sliced*
1	*large potato, peeled and cut into 1 cm (¹/₂ inch) pieces*
1	*garlic clove, finely chopped*
2 tsp	*fresh thyme, or ¹/₂ tsp dried thyme*
	freshly ground black pepper
³/₄ tsp	*salt*
1 litre/1³/₄ pints	*unsalted chicken stock*
³/₄ tsp	*ground cumin*
2 tbsp	*fresh lemon juice*
12.5 cl/4 fl oz	*single cream*
250 g/8 oz	*queen scallops, firm white connective tissue removed*

Put half of the butter into a 4 litre (7 pint) casserole. Add the broccoli, leeks, potato, garlic, thyme and some pepper. Cover the casserole with a lid or plastic film, then microwave the vegetables on high for 5 minutes.

Add the salt, stock, ³/₄ litre (1¹/₄ pints) of water and the cumin. Cover the dish leaving a corner open for the steam to escape, then microwave the mixture on high for 15 minutes, stirring every 5 minutes. Stir in the lemon juice and cook the mixture on high for 15 minutes more, stirring every 5 minutes. Let the casserole stand for 10 minutes before puréeing the mixture in batches in a blender or food processor. Return the purée to the casserole; then stir in the cream. Microwave the mixture on high until it is heated through—about 2 minutes.

In a bowl, microwave the remaining butter on high until it melts—about 30 seconds. Add the scallops and cook them on high for 30 seconds; stir the scallops, then cook them just until they turn opaque—about 30 seconds more.

Ladle the hot purée into heated individual soup plates; garnish each serving with some scallops and serve the soup immediately.

Pork and Bean Sprout Soup

Serves 4

Working time: about 30 minutes

Total time: about 1 hour

Calories 245, Protein 30g, Cholesterol 75mg, Total fat 5g,
Saturated fat 2g, Sodium 490mg

1/2 tsp	*Sichuan peppercorns, or freshly ground black pepper to taste*
500 g/1 lb	*lean pork, julienned*
1/4 tsp	*cayenne pepper*
1/4 tsp	*ground ginger*
2 tbsp	*Chinese black vinegar or balsamic vinegar*
1 litre/1³/₄ pints	*unsalted brown stock*
1	*onion, thinly sliced*
6	*garlic cloves, thinly sliced*
250 g/8 oz	*bean sprouts*
1.25 kg/2¹/₂ lb	*ripe tomatoes, skinned, seeded and chopped, or 800 g (28 oz) canned tomatoes, drained and crushed*
4 tbsp	*chopped fresh parsley*
2 tbsp	*low-sodium soy sauce or shoyu*

Toast the Sichuan peppercorns, if you are using them, in a heavy frying pan over medium-high heat until they smoke—about 2 minutes; using a mortar and pestle, grind them to a powder. Combine the pork with the ground peppercorns or black pepper, cayenne pepper, ginger and vinegar in a small bowl. Let the mixture stand at room temperature for 30 minutes.

Pour the stock into a 2 litre (3¹/₂ pint) glass bowl. Add the onion and garlic, and cover the bowl with a lid. Microwave the liquid on high for 10 minutes. Remove the bowl from the oven and stir the mixture. Cover the bowl again and cook the liquid on high for 10 minutes more.

Meanwhile, place the bean sprouts in a colander and blanch them by pouring about 2 litres (3¹/₂ pints) of boiling water over them. Set the bean sprouts aside.

Stir the pork and its marinade into the cooked broth. Microwave the mixture on high until it barely begins to boil, then cook on high for 3 minutes. Add the tomatoes, parsley, soy sauce and blanched bean sprouts. Cook the soup, uncovered, for 3 minutes more on high. Serve immediately.

Seafood Stew in Garlic-Tomato Sauce

Serves 6

Working (and total) time: about 1 hour

Calories 220, Protein 24g, Cholesterol 175mg, Total fat 5g, Saturated fat 1g, Sodium 305mg

1 kg/2 lb	*mussels, scrubbed and debearded*
12.5 cl/4 fl oz	*dry white wine*
1 tsp	*chopped fresh oregano, or $^{1}/_{4}$ tsp dried oregano*
	freshly ground black pepper
175 g/6 oz	*squid, cleaned*
500 g/1 lb	*cooked prawns, peeled*
	Garlic-tomato sauce
1	*onion, chopped*
4	*garlic cloves, finely chopped*
1 tsp	*chopped fresh oregano, or $^{1}/_{4}$ tsp dried oregano*
$^{1}/_{8}$ tsp	*cayenne pepper*
1	*lime, juice only*
1 tsp	*caster sugar*
1 tbsp	*virgin olive oil*
1.25 kg/2$^{1}/_{2}$ lb	*ripe tomatoes, skinned, seeded and chopped, or 800 g (28 oz) canned tomatoes, drained and chopped*
1	*sweet green pepper, seeded, deribbed and cut into thin strips*

Place half of the mussels, along with the wine, oregano and some black pepper, in a 2 litre (3$^{1}/_{2}$ pint) bowl. Cover the bowl with plastic film (leaving one corner open) or a lid and microwave the mussels on high, rotating the dish half way through the cooking time, until they open—about 5 minutes. Remove the opened mussels and set them aside; discard any that remain closed. Cook the other half of the mussels in the same way. Do not pour out the cooking liquid.

When the mussels are cool enough to handle, remove them from their shells, working over the bowl to catch their juices. Discard the shells and set the mussels aside. Strain the liquid through a sieve lined with muslin into a cup; discard the solids. Wash the cooking bowl in order to make the sauce in it.

To make the garlic-tomato sauce, put the onion, garlic, oregano, cayenne pepper, lime juice, sugar and oil into the bowl. Cover it and cook the mixture on high for 2 minutes. Add the tomatoes and the reserved liquid from the mussels and cook, covered, on high for 10 minutes, stirring half way through the cooking time. Reduce the heat to medium (50 per cent power) and cook the sauce for 10 minutes more, again stirring after 5 minutes.

While the sauce is cooking, prepare the squid. Slit one side of the pouch and lay it flat, skinned side down. Using a sharp knife, score the flesh diagonally in a cross-hatch pattern. Then cut the pouch into 4 cm (1$^{1}/_{2}$ inch) squares and set them aside.

Add the green pepper to the sauce and continue to cook the mixture on medium (50 per cent power) until the pepper is tender—about 5 minutes. Stir in the mussels, squid and prawns. Cook the dish on high for an additional 2 minutes and serve it hot.

Cauliflower Cheese Mould

Serves 6

Working (and total) time: about 50 minutes

Calories 185, Protein 11g, Cholesterol 100mg, Total fat 11g,
Saturated fat 6g, Sodium 270mg

1 kg/2 lb	*cauliflower florets*
45 g/1½ oz	*unsalted butter*
45 g/1½ oz	*plain flour*
30 cl/½ pint	*skimmed milk*
60 g/2 oz	*Parmesan cheese, grated*
2	*eggs, beaten*
½ tsp	*salt*
	freshly ground black pepper
¼ tsp	*grated nutmeg*
	strips of peeled sweet red pepper, for garnish
	watercress sprigs, for garnish

Put the cauliflower florets into a very large bowl, add 6 tablespoons of cold water, then cover the bowl with plastic film, pulling it back at one corner. Cook on high for 15 to 20 minutes, stirring every 5 minutes, until the cauliflower is cooked but still slightly firm. Meanwhile, grease a 20 cm (8 inch) round dish. Line the bottom with greased non-stick parchment paper.

Drain any excess water from the cauliflower florets, then process them briefly in a food processor until they are finely broken up but not puréed. Set aside.

Put the butter into a large bowl and microwave it on high for 30 seconds, until melted. Mix in the flour, then gradually stir in the milk. Cook on high for 4 minutes, stirring every minute with a wire whisk, until thick. Remove from the microwave and beat in the Parmesan, eggs, salt, pepper, nutmeg and cauliflower.

Carefully spoon the cauliflower mixture into the prepared dish and level the surface. Cover the dish with plastic film, leaving a corner open. Cook on high for 12 to 15 minutes, until set, giving the dish a quarter turn every 3 minutes.

Remove the cauliflower mould from the oven and allow it to stand for 5 minutes, then carefully turn it out on to a flat serving dish. Garnish with the sweet pepper strips and watercress sprigs. Serve cut into wedges.

EDITOR'S NOTE: To peel a sweet red pepper using the microwave, prick the pepper several times with a fork or skewer and place it on a double layer of paper towels in the oven. Microwave on high for 5 minutes, until soft, turning once. Transfer the pepper to a bowl and cover it with plastic film. Leave it to sweat for 5 to 10 minutes, then peel it.

Courgette and Tomato Clafoutis

CLAFOUTIS, TRADITIONALLY BLACK BAKED CHERRIES BAKED IN A SWEET
PANCAKE BATTER, IS A SPECIALITY OF THE LIMOUSIN DISTRICT OF
FRANCE. IN THIS SAVOURY ADAPTATION, VEGETABLES AND HERBS
REPLACE THE FRUIT.

Serves 4

Working (and total) time: about 45 minutes

Calories 120, Protein 9g, Cholesterol 110mg, Total fat 4g,
Saturated fat 1g, Sodium 270mg

2	*eggs*
30 g/1 oz	*wholemeal flour*
30 g/1 oz	*plain flour*
2 tbsp	*wheat germ*
30 cl/¹/₂ pint	*skimmed milk*
200 g/7 oz	*cherry tomatoes, pierced with a fine skewer*
250 g/8 oz	*courgettes, sliced into 1 cm (¹/₂ inch) rounds*
2	*fresh thyme sprigs, leaves only, chopped if large*
8	*large basil leaves, torn in strips*
¹/₂ tsp	*bottled peppercorns, drained and rinsed freshly ground green pepper (optional)*

In a bowl, combine the eggs with the plain and whole-
meal flours and 1 tablespoon of the wheat germ. Whisk
in the milk and salt. Set the batter aside to rest for 20
to 30 minutes.

Brush the base and sides of a 25 cm (10 inch) diameter shallow microwave dish with a little olive oil and
sprinkle evenly with the remaining wheat germ. Arrange the tomatoes and courgettes in the dish.

Stir the batter well, then mix in the herbs and peppercorns. Pour the mixture over the vegetables. Cover
the dish with plastic film, leaving one corner open.
Microwave on medium, stirring the contents of the
dish from time to time, until the edges of the batter
begin to set—3 to 5 minutes. Then microwave for a
further 10 minutes, giving the dish a quarter turn every
3 minutes. Remove the plastic film, place a layer of
absorbent paper towel lightly over the surface of the
clafoutis and cover it with a fresh piece of plastic
film. Allow the clafoutis to stand, covered, for 3 minutes.

The clafoutis should now be set in the centre. If it is
not, microwave it on medium for a further 2 to 3 minutes, then allow it to rest for 2 more minutes.

Serve the clafoutis warm, cut into wedges. Grind a
little green pepper over each portion if you like.

Salad-Filled Potato Pie

Serves 6

Working time: about 30 minutes

Total time: about 40 minutes

Calories 190, Protein 5g, Cholesterol 45mg, Total fat 4g,
Saturated fat 1g, Sodium 230mg

1 kg/2 lb	*large potatoes, scrubbed*
1 tbsp	*potato flour*
2 tbsp	*skimmed mllk*
3 cl/1 fl oz	*plain low-fat yoghurt*
45 g/1¹/₂ oz	*crème fraîche*
2 tbsp	*finely chopped fresh dill*
³/₄ tsp	*salt*
	freshly grated nutmeg
1 tsp	*safflower oil*
60 g/2 oz	*watercress leaves roughly chopped*
100 g/3¹/₂ oz	*cucumber, peeled and cut into 2.5 cm (1 inch) long bâtonnets*
200 g/7 oz	*tomatoes, skinned, seeded and chopped*
	freshly ground black pepper
¹/₂ tsp	*mild paprika*

Prick each of the potatoes all over with a fork and arrange them in a circle, on a double layer of paper towels, in the microwave. Microwave on high for 12 to 15 minutes, rotating the paper towels every 3 minutes, until the potatoes are cooked through. Leave the po-

tatoes to rest for a further 3 minutes, then peel them and mash them.

In a bowl, blend the potato flour with the milk, then beat in the egg, yoghurt, *crème fraîche*, dill, ¹/₂ teaspoon of the salt and some grated nutmeg. Beat this mixture into the mashed potato.

Brush a 25 by 16 cm (10 by 6 inch) baking dish with the safflower oil. Spread half of the potato mixture over the base and sides of the dish. Scatter the watercress over the potato to within 1 cm (¹/₂ inch) of the sides. Arrange the cucumber and the chopped tomatoes on top of the watercress. Sprinkle the filling with the remaining ¹/₄ teaspoon of salt and a generous grinding of black pepper.

Carefully spread the remaining potato over the filling to enclose it completely. Mark the surface with a fork and sift the paprika evenly over the top.

Cover the dish with plastic film, leaving two opposite corners open. Microwave on high for 7 to 10 minutes, giving the dish a quarter turn every 7 minutes, until heated through. Remove the pie from the oven and allow it to rest for a further 3 minutes. Serve the potato pie cut into squares.

EDITOR'S NOTES: To skin tomatoes in the microwave, pierce the skin once or twice, then microwave on high for about 45 seconds, until the skin starts to peel away.

Spiced Bean Medley

BEANS COOKED IN THE MICROWAVE TAKE ALMOST AS LONG AS WHEN
COOKED CONVENTIONALLY, BUT THEY HAVE THE ADVANTAGE THAT
HOWEVER LONG THEY COOK THEY DO NOT GO MUSHY.

Serves 6
Working time: about 20 minutes
Total time: about 2 hours and 40 minutes (includes soaking)
Calories 220, Protein 12g, Cholesterol 0mg, Total fat 4g,
Saturated fat 0g, Sodium 25mg

125 g/4 oz	dried red kidney beans, picked over
90 g/3 oz	dried pinto beans, picked over
60 g/2 oz	dried black kidney beans, picked over
30 g/1 oz	dried aduki beans, picked over
1 tbsp	safflower oil
2	garlic cloves, sliced
1	small fresh red chilli pepper, seeded and finely chopped
1	small fresh green chilli pepper, seeded and finely chopped
1	sweet red pepper, seeded, deribbed and cut into strips
500 g/1 lb	tomatoes, skinned, seeded and chopped

Put all the beans into a large casserole, pour in about 2 litres (3½ pints) of boiling water and microwave, un-covered, on high for 15 minutes. Stir the beans, then set them aside to soak for 1 hour.

Put the oil, garlic, onion, chilli peppers and sweet red pepper into a casserole and cook, uncovered, on high, for 3 minutes. Stir in the salt and the tomatoes, then set the sauce aside until needed.

After the beans have soaked, drain them and rinse them well in cold water. Return them to the casserole and cover them with fresh boiling water. Cook the beans, uncovered, on high for 30 minutes, then cook them on medium for a further 50 minutes. At the end of cooking, drain the beans and return them to the casserole, together with the sauce. Cook on high for 3 to 5 minutes, until thoroughly heated through. Stir the medley before serving it.

EDITOR'S NOTE: To skin tomatoes in the microwave, pierce the skin once or twice, then microwave on high for about 45 seconds, until the skin starts to peel away. The spiced bean medley may also be served cold, in which case a crisp green salad makes a good accompaniment.

Oriental Parchment Parcels

Serves 4

Working (and total) time: about 20 minutes

Calories 110, Protein 5g, Cholesterol 0mg, Total fat 8mg, Saturated fat 0g, Sodium 10mg

4 tsp	*sesame oil*
200 g/7 oz	*firm tofu, cut into 2 cm (³/₄ inch) cubes*
100 g/3¹/₂ oz	*fresh shiitake mushrooms, finely sliced*
75 g/2¹/₂ oz	*baby sweetcorn, cut into 2.5 cm (1 inch) lengths*
75 g/2¹/₂ oz	*courgettes, sliced*
60 g/2 oz	*young carrots, cut into thin ribbons with a vegetable peeler*
4 tsp	*low-sodium soy sauce or shoyu*
2	*large garlic cloves, halved or four small garlic cloves*
5 cm	*piece fresh ginger root, cut in half*

Take four sheets of greaseproof or non-stick parchment paper, each about 25 cm (10 inches) square, and brush the centres with 1 teaspoon of the oil.

Divide the tofu cubes and vegetables equally among the four pieces of paper, piling the ingredients on to the oiled section. In a small bowl mix the remaining oil with the soy sauce. Using a garlic press, crush the garlic and ginger and add the pulp and juices to the bowl, discarding any coarse fibres that may have been pushed through the press. Sprinkle a quarter of this mixture over each pile of vegetables.

Bring two facing edges of one of the paper sheets together above the vegetables, and make a double fold in the edges, to seal and join them. Then make a double fold in each of the two open ends, to seal the parcel completely. Prepare the other three parcels in the same way, and place all four in a wide shallow dish, arranging them towards the outside edges of the dish so that they will cook evenly.

Microwave on high for 4 to 5 minutes, until the vegetables are tender, giving the dish a quarter turn after each minute. Serve as soon as possible, keeping the parcels closed until the moment of serving.

Mushroom Quiche

Serves 4

Working time (and total) time: about 40 minutes

Calories 265, Protein 10g, Cholesterol 30mg, Total fat 14g, Saturated fat 6g, Sodium 120mg

125 g/4 oz	*wholemeal flour*
30 g/1 oz	*unsalted peanut butter*
30 g/1 oz	*unsalted butter, chilled*

Mushroom filling

175 g/6 oz	*fresh shiitake mushrooms*
175 g/6 oz	*oyster mushrooms*
15 g/¹/₂ oz	*unsalted butter*
15 g/¹/₂ oz	*wholemeal flour*
15 cl/¹/₄ pint	*skimmed milk*
1 tbsp	*chopped parsley*
¹/₄ tsp	*salt*
	freshly ground black pepper

To make pastry, put the flour into a mixing bowl and lightly rub in the peanut butter and butter, until the mixture resembles fine breadcrumbs. Using a round bladed knife to mix, add enough cold water to the flour mixture to form a fairly firm dough—about 3 to 4 tablespoons. Turn the dough out on to a work surface dusted with a little flour, and roll it out to line an 18 cm (7 inch) fluted flan dish. This kind of dough is quite crumbly, so use any trimmings to fill in the cracks. Chill the pastry case in the refrigerator for 5 minutes, then line it with a paper towel. Press the towel gently into the contours of the case. Microwave on high for 4 to 5 minutes, until the pastry looks dry.

For the filling, put the mushrooms into a bowl with 2 tablespoons of cold water. Cover with plastic film, leaving one corner open, and cook on high for 2 minutes. Remove from the oven and set aside. In a separate bowl, heat the butter on high for 15 to 20 seconds, or until melted. Stir in the flour and then whisk in the milk. Add the parsley and cook on high for 3 minutes, stirring every minute with a wire whisk. Season with the salt and some pepper, then add the mushrooms and cook on high, covered as before, for a further 3 minutes, stirring after the first minute.

Remove the paper towel from the pastry case, pour in the mushroom filling, and serve immediately.

EDITOR'S NOTE: If shiitake and oyster mushrooms are not available, you can use a mixture of small open cup mushrooms and button mushrooms instead.

Lasagne Layered with Spinach

Serves 8

Working time: about 20 minutes

Total time: about 1 hour and 15 minutes

Calories 300, Protein 20g, Cholesterol 40mg, Total fat 13g,
Saturated fat 8g, Sodium 410mg

8	*lasagne strips*
30 g/1 oz	*unsalted butter*
1	*medium onion, finely chopped*
2	*garlic cloves, finely chopped*
125 g/4 oz	*mushrooms, wiped clean and thinly sliced*
800 g/28 oz	*canned tomatoes, drained and coarsely chopped, the juice reserved*
4 tbsp	*tomato paste*
4 tbsp	*red wine*
1 tbsp	*chopped fresh oregano, or ¹/₂ tbsp dried oregano*
2 tbsp	*chopped fresh basil leaves, or 1 tbsp dried basil*
2 tbsp	*dark brown sugar*
¹/₂ tsp	*salt*
	freshly ground black pepper
2 tbsp	*freshly grated Parmesan cheese*
500 g/1 lb	*low-fat ricotta cheese*
1	*egg white*
500 g/1 lb	*fresh spinach, rinsed, stemmed, blanched in boiling water for 1 minute, squeezed dry and chopped*
250 g/¹/₂ lb	*low-fat mozzarella, thinly sliced*

To begin the sauce, put the butter in a 2 litre (3¹/₂ pint) glass bowl, cover it with a lid or plastic film, and microwave it on high until the butter is melted—about 1 minute. Add the onion, garlic and mushrooms, toss them until they are coated with the butter. Cover the bowl again and microwave it on medium high (70 per cent power) for 2 minutes. Add the tomatoes, the reserved juice, the tomato paste, wine, oregano, basil, sugar, salt and some pepper, and stir well. Cover the bowl with a paper towel and microwave the contents on high for 12 minutes, stirring every 4 minutes. Stir the Parmesan cheese and set the mixture aside.

In a smaller bowl, mix the ricotta with the egg white and some more pepper. Add the spinach and mix well.

Assemble the lasagne in a 25 cm (10 inch) square shallow baking dish. First spread 12.5 cl (4 fl oz) of the sauce evenly over the bottom of the dish. Lay uncooked lasagne strips side by side in the sauce, then cover them with a thin layer of the spinach mixture and a layer of mozzarella slices. Repeat the layering process and spread half of the remaining sauce on top of the cheese, then cover it with the remaining lasagne, the rest of the spinach mixture and the last of the mozzarella. Top the dish with the remaining sauce and cover it with plastic film, leaving a corner open; microwave it on high for 6 minutes, then on medium high (70 per cent power) for 20 minutes more. Let the lasagne stand for 15 minutes before serving it.

Fettuccine alla Carbonara

Serves 4
Working (and total) time: about 20 minutes
Calories 440, Protein 19g, Cholesterol 90mg, Total fat 18g, Saturated fat 8g, Sodium 470mg

250 g/8 oz	*fettuccine*
100 g/3¹/₂ oz	*lean rindless back bacon rashers*
15 cl/¹/₄ pint	*semi-skimmed milk*
10 cl/3¹/₂ fl oz	*low-fat single cream*
15 g/¹/₂ oz	*Parmesan cheese, freshly grated*
1	*egg and 1 egg white*
	freshly ground black pepper
15 g/¹/₂ oz	*unsalted butter*
2	*garlic cloves, crushed*
	finely chopped parsley, to garnish

Cover a large heatproof plate with a double thickness of absorbent kitchen paper. Arrange the bacon rashers in a single layer on the paper, then cover them with a double thickness of absorbent paper. Microwave on high for 2 to 2¹/₂ minutes until the bacon is cooked. Chop the bacon into small pieces and set aside.

Pour 2¹/₂ litres (4 pints) of boiling water into a large bowl, add 1¹/₂ teaspoons of salt and the fettuccine. Microwave on high for 10 to 12 minutes until the pasta is *al dente*, stirring every 3 minutes. Drain the fettuccine, cover and keep warm.

In a small bowl, lightly whisk together the cream, milk, Parmesan cheese, egg and egg white. Season with pepper, and set aside.

Put the butter into a large bowl and microwave on high for 30 seconds, until melted. Add the garlic and bacon, and microwave for a further 1 minute.

Add the egg and cream mixture to the garlic and bacon. Microwave for 2 to 2¹/₂ minutes, stirring every 30 seconds until the mixture is very hot, and slightly thickened. Add the pasta and mix well. Pour into a large warm serving bowl, sprinkle with parsley and serve immediately.

Egg Noodles with Beef and Mushrooms in a Creamy Sauce

THIS RECIPE IS A LOW-CALORIE VARIATION
OF THE CLASSIC BEEF STROGANOFF.

Serves 4

Working (and total) time: about 20 minutes

Calories 435, Protein 26g, Cholesterol 100mg, Total fat 14g,
Saturated fat 7g, Sodium 445mg

250 g/8 oz	wide egg noodles
2 tsp	safflower oil
15 g/^{1}/$_2$ oz	unsalted butter
250 g/8 oz	mushrooms, wiped clean, stems trimmed, thinly sliced
1	small onion, thinly sliced, the layers separated
250 g/8 oz	beef fillet, cut into thin strips about 5 cm (2 inches) long and 1 cm (^{1}/$_2$ inch) wide
1	garlic clove, finely chopped
1 tsp	dry mustard, mixed with 1 tsp water
1^1/$_2$ tbsp	paprika, preferably Hungarian
^{1}/$_2$ tsp	salt
	freshly ground black pepper
4 tbsp	soured cream
12.5 cl/4 fl oz	plain low-fat yoghurt
4 tbsp	coarsely chopped chives

Cook the noodles in the conventional manner: put them into 3 litres (5 pints) of boiling water on the stove top with 1^1/$_2$ teaspoons of salt. Start testing them after 7 minutes and cook them until they are al dente. Drain the noodles, toss them with the oil, and set them aside.

While the noodles are cooking, put the butter in a 2 litre (3^1/$_2$ pint) bowl and cover the bowl with a lid or plastic film. Microwave the butter on high for 30 seconds. Add the mushrooms and onion, and gently toss them until they are coated with the butter. Cover the bowl again and microwave the contents on medium high (70 per cent power) for 2 minutes. Add the beef strips, garlic, mustard, 1 tablespoon of the paprika, the ^{1}/$_2$ teaspoon of salt and a generous grinding of black pepper to the mushroom-onion mixture. Cover again and microwave on medium high (70 per cent power) for 5 minutes, stirring the mixture half way through the cooking time. Remove the bowl and drain off the liquid that has accumulated in the bottom.

Add the noodles, soured cream and yoghurt to the bowl; stir well, cover the bowl and microwave it on high for 2 minutes, stirring after 1 minute. Transfer the mixture to a serving dish. Sprinkle the remaining paprika and the chives over the top and serve the dish hot.

Penne with Provençal Vegetables

Serves 4

Working (and total) time: about 40 minutes

Calories 335, Protein 11g, Cholesterol 5mg, Total fat 7g,
Saturated fat 1g, Sodium 185mg

250 g/8 oz *penne (or other short, tubular pasta)*
250 g/8 oz *aubergine*
     2 *courgettes*
     2 *sweet red peppers, seeded, deribbed*
       and cut into 1 cm ($^1/_2$ inch) squares
     3 *garlic cloves, peeled and thinly sliced*
  2 tbsp *chopped fresh parsley*
  $^1/_4$ tsp *fresh oregano, or $^1/_8$ tsp dried oregano*
  $^1/_4$ tsp *finely chopped fresh rosemary, or $^1/_8$*
     tsp dried rosemary, crushed
  $^1/_4$ tsp *fresh thyme, or $^1/_8$ tsp dried thyme*
  $^1/_8$ tsp *fennel seeds*
  $^1/_4$ tsp *salt*
     freshly ground black pepper
  2 tbsp *virgin olive oil*
$^1/_2$ litre/16 fl oz *unsalted chicken stock*
$^1/_4$ litre/8 fl oz *unsalted tomato juice*

Halve the aubergine and the courgettes lengthwise,
then cut them lengthwise again into wedges about 1
cm ($^1/_2$ inch) wide. Slice the wedges into 2.5 cm (1
inch) long pieces. Put the pieces in a baking dish along
with the red pepper, garlic, parsley, oregano, rosemary,
thyme, fennel seeds, salt and some pepper. Cover
the dish and microwave it on high for 2 minutes.
Rotate the dish half a turn and microwave it on high
until the vegetables are barely tender—about 2 minutes more. Stir in the oil and set aside while you
cook the pasta.

In a deep bowl, combine the penne, stock and tomato juice. If necessary, add just enough water to
immerse the pasta in liquid. Cover the bowl, leaving
one corner open if using plastic film, and microwave it
on high, rotating the bowl a quarter turn and stirring
the pasta every 2 minutes, until it is *al dente*—about
15 minutes in all. With a slotted spoon, transfer the
pasta to the baking dish with the vegetable mixture
and stir to combine. Pour about half of the pasta cooking liquid into the dish, then cover the dish and microwave it on high for 2 minutes more to heat it through.
Serve at once.

Cannelloni with Cottage Cheese and Courgettes

TO ENSURE THAT THE PASTA WILL COOK COMPLETELY THROUGH, THE SAUCE MUST BE WARM WHEN YOU ASSEMBLE THE DISH.

Serves 6
Working time: about 35 minutes
Total time: about 1 hour and 30 minutes
Calories 380, Protein 24g, Cholesterol 30mg, Total fat 11g, Saturated fat 7g, Sodium 590mg

12	cannelloni tubes (about 250 g/8 oz)
30 g/1 oz	unsalted butter
3	large shallots, finely chopped (about 3 tbsp)
2	garlic cloves, finely chopped
1	medium carrot, peeled and coarsely grated
1	medium courgette, sliced into thin rounds
800 g/28 oz	canned tomatoes, drained and coarsely chopped, the juice reserved
4 tbsp	tomato paste
1 tbsp	chopped fresh oregano, or 1/2 tbsp dried oregano
2 tbsp	chopped fresh basil leaves, or 1 tbsp dried basil
2 tbsp	dark brown sugar
	freshly ground black pepper
1/4 tsp	salt
350 g/12 oz	low-fat cottage cheese
125 g/4 oz	low-fat mozzarella, coarsely grated
3	egg whites
3 tbsp	chopped fresh parsley
60 g/2 oz	Parmesan cheese, freshly grated
	fresh basil sprigs for garnish (optional)

Put the butter in a 2 litre (3 1/2 pint) bowl. Cover the bowl with a lid or plastic film and microwave it on high until the butter melts—about 30 seconds. Add the shallots, garlic, carrot and courgette; toss the vegetables to coat them with the butter, then microwave them on medium high (70 per cent power) for 4 minutes. Add the tomatoes and their juice, the tomato paste, oregano, basil, brown sugar, some pepper and the salt, and stir well. Cover the bowl loosely and microwave the contents on medium high (70 per cent power) for 12 minutes, stirring every 4 minutes. Set the sauce aside.

To make the filling, stir together the cottage cheese, mozzarella, egg whites, parsley and the Parmesan cheese. Using a small spoon or a piping bag with no nozzle, carefully fill the tubes with the mixture.

To assemble the dish, first reheat the sauce, if necessary, then spread half of it over the bottom of a shallow baking dish. Lay the filled cannelloni tubes in the sauce in a single layer and pour the remaining sauce over them. Cover the dish and microwave it on high for 10 minutes, then turn each tube over. Cover the dish again and microwave it on medium high for 17 minutes more. Uncover the dish and let the cannelloni stand for 12 to 15 minutes. Garnish with sprigs of fresh basil if desired.

Orange-Ginger Trout

Serves 8

Working time: about 30 minutes
Total time: about 1 hour
Calories 250, Protein 28g, Cholesterol 85mg, Total fat 10g,
Saturated fat 2g, Sodium 155mg

4	trout, about 500 g (1 lb) each, filleted and skinned
2	oranges, the grated rind and juice of 1 reserved, the other left whole
1 tbsp	finely chopped fresh ginger root
2	shallots, finely chopped
¹/₄ litre/8 fl oz	dry white vine
1 kg/2 lb	spinach, washed and stemmed
1	garlic clove, finely chopped
¹/₄ tsp	salt
	freshly ground black pepper
15 g/¹/₂ oz	unsalted butter

Rinse the fillets under cold running water and pat them dry with paper towels. In a 20 cm (8 inch) round baking dish, combine the grated orange rind, orange juice, ginger, shallots and wine. Place the fillets in the liquid and let them marinate at room temperature for 30 minutes.

Put half of the spinach, with the water still clinging to it, and half of the garlic in a bowl and microwave them on high for 3 minutes. Repeat the process to cook the remaining spinach and garlic, set both of the batches aside.

Meanwhile, peel and section the whole orange, and remove the outer membrane from each segment.

Remove the fillets from their marinade. Fold each fillet loosely in thirds, with the boned side out and the ends tucked under the middle, envelope-fashion. Add the salt and some pepper to the marinade and stir it well. Replace the folded fillets in the marinade, with their sides not touching, and microwave them on high until they are slightly translucent—5 to 7 minutes. Remove the fillets from the cooking liquid and set them aside.

Strain the liquid into a small bowl and microwave it on high, uncovered, until it is reduced by half—about 5 minutes. Add the butter and cook the mixture for 2 minutes more.

Arrange the spinach in an even layer in the baking dish. Place the folded fillets on the spinach bed and top each one with an orange segment. Return the dish to the oven and microwave it on high until it is warmed through—about 90 seconds. Pour the sauce over all and serve immediately.

Soused Norway Haddock

SOUSED (PICKLED) FISH CAN BE MADE UP TO 24 HOURS IN ADVANCE AND REFRIGERATED. ITS FLAVOUR IMPROVES WITH TIME.

Serves 8 as a first course
Working time: about 20 minutes
Total time: about 1 hour and 20 minutes
Calories 65, Protein 11g, Cholesterol 25mg, Total fat 2g,
Saturated fat 0g, Sodium 65mg

500 g/1 lb	*Norway haddock fillets (or herring), skin on*
1	*small onion, sliced, rings separated*
1	*small carrot, quartered and sliced*
1	*bay leaf*
$1/2$ tsp	*coriander seeds*
$1/4$ tsp	*mustard seeds*
$1/4$ tsp	*celery seeds*
8	*black pepper corns*
4 tbsp	*cider vinegar*
$1/4$ tsp	*salt*

In a 30 cm (12 inch) round glass dish, combine the onion, carrot, bay leaf, coriander seeds, mustard seeds, celery seeds and peppercorns with $1/4$ litre (8 fl oz) of water. Cover the dish and microwave it on high for 3 minutes. Rotate the dish half a turn and cook the contents for 2 minutes more. Remove the plate from the oven and let it stand for 3 minutes.

Add the vinegar and salt to the mixture and stir gently to dissolve the salt. Rinse the fillets under cold running water. Place the fillets in the dish, with their skin sides up and their edges not touching. Cook the fish on high, uncovered, for 2 minutes. Turn the plate half a turn and cook until the fish feels firm to the touch—1 to 2 minutes more. Refrigerate the fish, in its liquid, for at least 1 hour. Serve the soused fish chilled or at room temperature.

Prawn Teriyaki

Serves 4

Working time: about 20 minutes

Total time: about 30 minutes

Calories 125, Protein 17g, Cholesterol 130mg, Total fat 1g,
Saturated fat 0g, Sodium 405mg

500 g/1 lb	*large raw prawns, peeled and deveined*
4 tbsp	*sweet sherry*
2 tbsp	*low-sodium soy sauce or shoyu*
1 tsp	*rice vinegar*
1	*garlic clove, finely chopped*
1	*slice wholemeal bread*
1 tsp	*cornflour*
12.5 cl/4 fl oz	*fish stock or dry white wine*
1	*carrot peeled and julienned*
3	*spring onions, trimmed and cut into 5 cm (2 inch) pieces, the pieces thinly sliced lengthwise*

Combine the sherry, soy sauce, vinegar and garlic in a bowl. Add the prawns and stir gently to coat them evenly. Marinate the prawns in the refrigerator for 20 minutes, stirring them from time to time.

Microwave the slice of bread on high for 2 minutes. Place the bread in a polythene bag and crush it into crumbs with a rolling pin.

Mix the cornflour with 1 tablespoon of the stock or wine. Strain the marinade into a glass bowl; stir in all but 2 tablespoons of the remaining stock or wine, along with the cornflour mixture. Microwave this sauce on high for 3 minutes. Stir the sauce until it is smooth, then set it aside.

Dip the prawns into the breadcrumbs to coat them on one side. Arrange the prawns, coated side up, in a shallow dish. Pour in the remaining stock or wine. Cover the dish and microwave it on high for 3 minutes. Rearrange the prawns, turning any uncooked pieces towards the edge of the dish.

Stir the carrot and spring onion strips into the sauce; pour the sauce around the prawns. Cover the dish again and cook it on medium high (70 per cent power) for 2 minutes. Allow the prawns to stand, covered, for another 2 minutes before transferring them to a serving dish. Spoon the sauce and vegetables around the prawns and serve immediately.

Crab Meat with Tomatoes, Mushrooms and Garlic

Serves 4
Working (and total) time: about 25 minutes
Calories 215, Protein 22g, Cholesterol 85mg, Total fat 5g, Saturated fat 1g, Sodium 245mg

500 g/1 lb	*crab meat, picked over*
250 g/¹/₂ lb	*mushrooms, wiped clean and sliced*
6	*shallots, finely chopped*
6	*garlic cloves, finely chopped*
6 tbsp	*dry sherry*
6 tbsp	*dry white wine*
¹/₈ tsp	*crushed red pepper flakes*
500 g/1 lb	*ripe tomatoes, skinned, seeded and chopped*
2 tbsp	*chopped fresh parsley*
1 tbsp	*virgin olive oil*

Combine the mushrooms, shallots, garlic, sherry, wine and crushed red pepper flakes in a baking dish. Cover and microwave on high for 8 minutes, stirring once mid-way through the cooking time. Add the crab meat, tomatoes, parsley and oil, and toss well. Cover the dish tightly, microwave on high for 2 minutes and serve immediately. (If you prefer, spoon individual portions into ceramic or natural crab shells before serving.)

Haddock with Endive and Bacon

Serves 4

Working (and total) time: about 20 minutes

Calories 150, Protein 24g, Cholesterol 70mg, Total fat 3g,
Saturated fat 1g, Sodium 270mg

500 g/1 lb	haddock fillets (or cod or coley)
2	garlic cloves, finely chopped
2 tbsp	fresh lemon juice
1 tsp	fresh rosemary, or 1/4 tsp dried rosemary, crumbled
	freshly ground black pepper
2	rashers streaky bacon, rind removed
1	endive (about 500 g/1 lb), trimmed, washed and cut into 2.5 cm (1 inch) pieces
1/8 tsp	salt

Rinse the haddock under cold running water and pat it dry with paper towels. Cut it into four serving pieces. Rub the fish with half of the garlic, 1 tablespoon of the lemon juice, the rosemary and a generous grinding of pepper. Set the fish aside.

Cut the rashers in half crosswise and put them in the bottom of a large dish. Microwave the bacon on high until done but not crisp—about 2 minutes. Lay a strip of bacon on top of each piece of fish.

Add the remaining garlic to the bacon fat in the dish. Add the endive to the dish with the remaining lemon juice, the salt and some pepper. Toss the endive to distribute the seasonings, then mound it in the centre of the dish. Microwave the dish on high for 2 minutes. Briefly toss the endive again and then microwave it on high until it wilts—about 2 minutes more.

Lay the fish on top of the endive. Microwave the fish on medium (50 per cent power) until the flesh is opaque—5 to 6 minutes. Remove the dish from the oven and spoon the juices that have collected in the bottom into a small saucepan. Boil the juices rapidly until only 2 tablespoons of liquid remain; pour the sauce over the fish and serve at once.

Chicken Stew
with Soufflé Topping

Serves 4

Working time: about 30 minutes

Total time: about 50 minutes

Calories 280, Protein 26g, Cholesterol 55mg, Total fat 700g,
Saturated fat 2g, Sodium 590mg

4	*chicken thighs, skinned*
500 g/1 lb	*butternut squash, marrow or sweet potatoes*
17.5 cl/6 fl oz	*evaporated milk*
1/8 tsp	*grated nutmeg*
3/4 tsp	*salt*
	freshly ground black pepper
1 tsp	*fresh thyme, or 1/2 tsp dried thyme*
1	*onion, finely chopped*
1	*stick celery, finely chopped*
2 tbsp	*tomato paste*
75 g/2 1/2 oz	*shelled peas*
1 tsp	*unsalted butter*
6	*egg whites*

Prick the squash, marrow or sweet potatoes in three or four spots and place on a paper towel in the microwave oven. Cook on high for 10 to 12 minutes. Remove from the oven, cover with a paper towel, and allow to stand until tender when pierced with a fork—

5 to 11 minutes. Cut the vegetables in half lengthwise, discarding any seeds, and scoop the pulp into a food process or blender. Add the milk, nutmeg, 1/2 teaspoon of salt and a little pepper; purée until smooth.

Rub the thighs with the thyme and some more pepper. In a 1.5 litre (2 1/2 pint) soufflé dish, combine the onion, celery, tomato paste, the remaining salt and a bit more pepper. Put the dish in the microwave oven and cook on high for 2 minutes. Stir the mixture, then add the chicken thighs, with their thicker ends facing the edges of the dish. Cook on high for 4 minutes. Turn each piece of chicken to expose the other side, then mound the peas in the centre. Rub the inside of the soufflé dish with the butter.

Transfer the purée to a large mixing bowl. If you a using a food processor, thoroughly wash and dry its work bowl. Whip the egg whites in the processor or with an electric mixer until they form stiff peaks. Stir about one quarter of the egg whites into the purée to lighten it, then fold in the remaining egg whites.

Add the mixture to the soufflé dish, filling it to the top. Microwave on medium low for 18 to 20 minutes, turning the dish a quarter turn every 5 minutes; the top of the soufflé will crack slightly when it is done. Serve the soufflé immediately, while it is still puffy.

Chicken in a Tortilla Pie

Serves 4

Working time: about 20 minutes

Total time: about 30 minutes

Calories 550, Protein 54g, Cholesterol 170mg, Total fat 29g, Saturated fat 12g, Sodium 395mg

1.5 kg/3 lb	*chicken, wings removed, the rest skinned and quartered*
12.5 cl/4 fl oz	*unsalted chicken stock*
1/4 tsp	*ground coriander seeds*
1/8 tsp	*cayenne pepper*
1/4 tsp	*ground cumin*
1	*sweet green pepper, seeded, deribbed and finely chopped*
4	*spring onions, finely chopped*
1/4 tsp	*dried oregano*
1 tbsp	*virgin olive oil*
	freshly ground black pepper
175 g/6 oz	*low-sodium cheddar or Emmenthal cheese, grated*
2	*(25 cm/10 inch) flour tortillas*
1/8 tsp	*chilli powder*

Salsa

2	*large ripe tomatoes, skinned, seeded and finely chopped*
1 or 2	*hot green chilli peppers, seeded and very finely chopped*
2	*garlic cloves, finely chopped*
1	*lime, juice only*
1 tbsp	*chopped fresh coriander or parsley*
1/4 tsp	*salt*
	freshly ground black pepper

Place the chicken pieces in a baking dish with the meatier part of each piece towards the edge of the dish. Pour in the stock, and sprinkle the chicken with the coriander, cayenne pepper and 1/8 teaspoon of the cumin. Cover the dish with greaseproof paper and microwave on high for 10 minutes; half way through the cooking time, turn the pieces over. Remove the breasts from the dish and microwave the leg quarters for 2 minutes more. Then let the chicken stand in the cooking liquid until it is cool enough to handle. Discard the liquid and shred the meat with your fingers.

Combine the green pepper, spring onions, oregano, oil, black pepper and the remaining cumin in a bowl. Cover the bowl tightly with plastic film. Cook for 2 minutes on high, then remove the bowl from the oven and mix in the shredded chicken.

In a separate mixing bowl, stir together the salsa ingredients. Add 12.5 cl (4 fl oz) of the salsa and half of the cheese to the chicken mixture. Place a tortilla on a large plate, cover it with the chicken mixture and put the other tortilla on top. Sprinkle the pie with the remaining cheese and the chilli powder. Microwave on high until the cheese melts—about 3 minutes. Cut the pie into wedges and serve it with the remaining salsa.

Chicken Parmesan

Serves 4

Working time: about 15 minutes

Total time: about 40 minutes

Calories 370, Protein 33g, Cholesterol 95mg, Total fat 17g, Saturated fat 5g, Sodium 695mg

8	chicken drumsticks, skinned, rinsed and patted dry
1	small onion, chopped
1	apple, peeled, cored and finely grated
1 tbsp	safflower oil
35 cl/12 fl oz	puréed tomatoes
2 tbsp	tomato paste
2 tbsp	Madeira
1	garlic clove, finely chopped
1 tbsp	chopped fresh basil, or 1 tsp dried basil
1/4 tsp	dried oregano
	freshly ground black pepper
45 g/1 1/2 oz	cornflakes, crushed
60 g/2 oz	Parmesan cheese, freshly grated
12.5 cl/4 fl oz	plain low-fat yoghurt

Combine the onion and apple with the oil in a bowl. Cover with a paper towel and microwave on high for 1 minute. Stir in the puréed tomatoes, tomato paste, Madeira, garlic, basil, oregano and some pepper. Cover the bowl with a paper towel again and microwave on medium (50 per cent power) for 9 minutes, stirring the sauce three times during the cooking. Remove the bowl from the oven and let it stand.

While the sauce is cooking, prepare the drumsticks. Sprinkle them with some pepper. Mix the cornflake crumbs and the Parmesan cheese. Dip the drumsticks into the yoghurt, then dredge them in the crumbcheese mixture, coating them evenly. Arrange the drumsticks on a microwave roasting rack with the meatier parts towards the outside of the rack. Microwave on high for 15 minutes, turning the dish once half way through the cooking time. Remove the drumsticks and let them stand for 7 minutes; then arrange them on a serving platter. Reheat the sauce on high for 1 minute and pour some of it over the chicken. Pass the remaining sauce separately.

Barbecued Chicken

PRECOOKING THE CHICKEN IN THE MICROWAVE ALLOWS FOR A DRAMATIC REDUCTION IN GRILLING TIME.

Serves 4

Working time: about 20 minutes

Total time: about 40 minutes

Calories 345, Protein 42g, Cholesterol 125mg, Total fat 11g, Saturated fat 3g, Sodium 390mg

1.5 kg/3 lb	chicken, wings and back bone removed, the rest skinned and cut into serving pieces
1	small onion, chopped
1	garlic clove, finely chopped
1/4 tsp	safflower oil
1/4 litre	puréed tomatoes
1 tbsp	cider vinegar
2 tbsp	chutney
4 drops	Tabasco sauce
2 tbsp	dark brown sugar
1/4 tsp	dry mustard
	freshly ground black pepper

Light the charcoal in a barbecue grill about 30 minutes before grilling time.

To prepare the barbecue sauce, combine the onion, garlic and oil in a bowl. Cover with plastic film and microwave on high for 2 minutes. Add the puréed tomatoes, vinegar, chutney, Tabasco sauce, brown sugar, mustard and pepper, and stir well. Cover the bowl with a paper towel and microwave on medium high (70 per cent power) for 3 minutes. Stir the sauce again and microwave on medium high for 3 minutes more. Remove the sauce from the oven and let it stand while you precook the chicken.

Place the chicken pieces on a microwave roasting rack with their meatier portions towards the outside of the rack. Microwave the chicken on high for 6 minutes aside any pieces that have turned from pink to white, then rearrange the remaining pieces with their uncooked portions towards the outside of the rack. Continue to microwave on high for periods of 2 minutes, removing the pieces that turn white.

Brush the chicken with the barbecue sauce. Grill the pieces over the hot coals for approximately 10 minutes, turning them once during the cooking and basting them often with the remaining sauce.

Roast Turkey with Tarragon-Cream Sauce

Serves 12

Working time: about 30 minutes

Total time: about 1 hour and 30 minutes

Calories 305, Protein 45g, Cholesterol 90mg, Total fat 12g, Saturated fat 4g, Sodium 255mg

5.5 kg/12 lb	turkey, rinsed and patted dry
½ tsp	salt
1	onion, chopped
2 tbsp	low-sodium soy sauce, or naturally fermented shoyu
1 tsp	paprika
1 tbsp	virgin olive oil
12.5 cl/4 fl oz	single cream
2 tsp	chopped fresh tarragon, or chopped watercress
	freshly ground black pepper
1 tbsp	cornflour, mixed with 2 tbsp water

Rub the cavity of the turkey with ¼ teaspoon of the salt and put the chopped onion inside. Tie the legs together and tuck the wing tips under the bird. Cover the wings and the ends of the drumsticks with small bits of foil.

Combine the soy sauce, paprika and oil in a small bowl. Brush the underside of the turkey with about half of this mixture. Put the turkey in an oven cooking bag. Draw the bag closed, leaving a small opening for steam to escape. Secure the bag with a plastic strip or elastic band, not a metal twist tie. Place the turkey breast side down in a large rectangular dish and microwave it on high for 15 minutes. Rotate half a turn and cook the bird on high for 15 minutes more before removing it from the oven.

Pour the accumulated juices from the bag into a saucepan and set it aside; the juices will form the base for the sauce. Remove the foil from the wings and drumsticks. Turn the turkey breast side up and brush the wings and breast with the remaining soy sauce mixture.

Close the bag loosely once more and microwave the turkey on high for 15 minutes. Rotate the dish half a turn and cook on high for a final 15 minutes.

Remove the bird from the oven. Pour the additional roasting juices into the saucepan with the reserved juices. Let the turkey stand for 20 minutes, then test for doneness by piercing a thigh with the tip of a sharp knife; the juices should run clear. If they do not, microwave the bird on high for 5 to 10 minutes more.

During the standing time, prepare the sauce. Spoon as much fat as possible from the surface of the reserved roasting juices; there should be about ½ litre (16 fl oz). Bring the liquid to the boil on the stove top and cook rapidly until it is reduced to 35 cl (12 fl oz)—5 to 10 minutes. Add the cream, the tarragon or watercress, the remaining salt and some pepper. Return the liquid to the boil. Whisk the cornflour mixture into the sauce and cook until the sauce boils and thickens slightly—about 1 minute. Pour the sauce into a sauceboat; carve the turkey and serve.

EDITOR'S NOTE: If you use a frozen turkey you may find that it will render more juice than a fresh one; either discard the excess juice or reserve it for another use. Although this recipe calls for a 5.5 kg (12 lb) turkey, you can easily cook a bird as large as 7 kg (15 lb) in the microwave. Enclose the turkey in an oven cooking bag and microwave it on high for 5 minutes per 500 g (1 lb), turning the dish at three regular intervals during cooking and turning the bird over half way through. Avoid buying pre-basted turkeys for microwaving: their pockets of fat may explode during cooking. The pop-out thermometers imbedded in some turkeys will not be activated until the end of the standing time. Thawing a turkey in the microwave is not recommended.

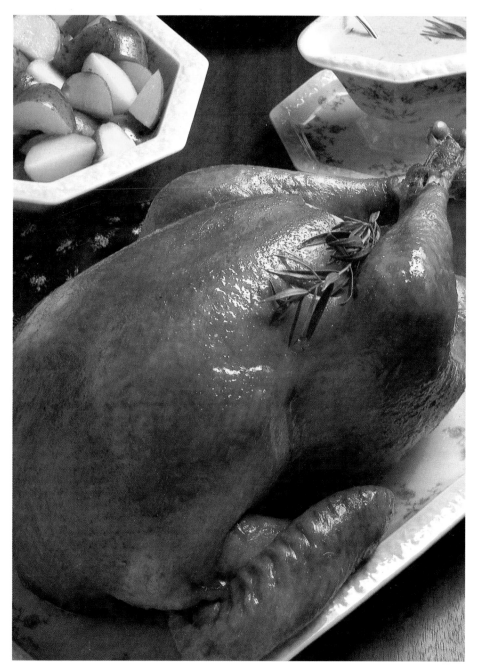

Turkey Ring

Serves 6

Working time: about 20 minutes

Total time: about 35 minutes

Calories 265, Protein 23g, Cholesterol 45mg, Total fat 3g, Saturated fat 12g, Sodium 315mg

500 g/1 lb	*turkey breast meat, cut into 5 cm (2 inch) cubes*
1	*small onion, finely chopped*
3 tbsp	*virgin olive oil, plus 1 tsp*
75 g/2¹/₂ oz	*dry breadcrumbs*
17.5 cl/6 fl oz	*semi-skimmed milk*
12.5 cl/4 fl oz	*plain low-fat yoghurt*
4 tbsp	*Parmesan cheese, freshly grated*
2 tbsp	*chopped fresh basil, or 1 tsp dried marjoram*
	freshly ground black pepper
1	*green courgette, julienned*
1	*yellow squash or courgette, julienned*
1	*sweet red pepper, julienned*
2	*garlic cloves, finely chopped*
¹/₄ tsp	*salt*

Combine the onion and 3 tablespoons of the oil in a small bowl. Cover lightly with plastic film and microwave on high until the onions are translucent—about 3 minutes. Uncover the onions and let them cool.

Mince the turkey in a food processor and mix in the breadcrumbs, milk and yoghurt. Add the onion, cheese, 1 tablespoon of the basil or ¹/₂ teaspoon of the marjoram, and some pepper. Operate the processor in short bursts to combine the ingredients.

With your hands, press the turkey mixture round the edges of a round dish 25 cm (10 inches) in diameter, forming a ring with a 10 cm (4 inch) diameter hollow at the centre. Cover tightly with plastic film, leaving a corner open for steam to escape, and microwave on high for 6 minutes, turning the dish a quarter turn every 2 minutes. Let the turkey ring stand while you cook the vegetables.

Combine the courgette, squash and red pepper in a bowl with the remaining oil, the remaining basil or marjoram, the garlic, salt and some pepper. Cover with plastic film and microwave on high for 4 minutes, stirring once half way through the cooking time. Arrange some of the vegetables in a thin band around the outside of the turkey ring and mound the remaining vegetables in the centre. Serve hot.

EDITOR'S NOTE: The turkey ring may be assembled in advance and then reheated for serving. To reheat the dish, cover it with plastic film or greaseproof paper and microwave it on medium high (70 percent power) for 4 minutes, turning once.

Stewed Fennel with Ham

Serves 4

Working time: about 5 minutes

Total time: about 20 minutes

Calories 130, Protein 8g, Cholesterol 30mg, Total fat 10g, Saturated fat 4g, Sodium 315mg

125 g/4 oz	ham, trimmed of fat
8	fennel bulbs
1 tbsp	finely chopped fresh thyme, or 1 tsp dried thyme
12.5 cl/4 fl oz	white wine
4 tbsp	unsalted vegetable stock
	freshly ground black pepper
30 g/1 oz	unsalted butter (optional)

Cut a thin slice off the root of each fennel bulb and trim off the tops of the stems; reserve the feathery fronds.

Put the fennel bulbs, thyme, white wine, vegetable stock, some freshly ground black pepper and the butter, if you are using it, into a dish. Cover and microwave on high until the fennel is cooked through—about 15 minutes.

Meanwhile, cut the ham into fine dice, and add it to the dish 1 minute before the end of the cooking time. Serve garnished with the feathery tops of the fennel, torn into small pieces.

EDITOR'S NOTE: Chicory or onions can be substituted for the fennel bulbs with equally good results. Allow two whole vegetables per person and cook for only 10 minutes; garnish with chopped parsley.

Cider Pork

Serves 6
Working time: about 25 minutes
Total time: about 4 hours and 30 minutes (includes marinating)
Calories 195, Protein 10g, Cholesterol 70mg, Total fat 10g, Saturated fat 4g, Sodium 80mg

750 g/1¹/₂ lb	*pork fillet, trimmed of fat and cut into 2.5 cm (1 inch) cubes*
1	*garlic clove crushed*
1 tbsp	*walnut oil*
15 cl/¹/₄ pint	*medium dry cider*
1	*orange, grated rind and juice*
2 tsp	*fresh lemon juice*
1 tbsp	*fresh thyme, or 1 tsp dried thyme*
¹/₂ tsp	*grated fresh ginger root*
¹/₂ tsp	*freshly ground black pepper*
4 tsp	*arrowroot dissolved in 3 tbsp cider*

In a large casserole, mix together all the ingredients except the pork and the arrowroot mixture. Stir in the pork, cover and leave to marinate in the refrigerator for 4 to 6 hours. Stir the meat once or twice during this time to make sure the cubes are evenly soaked.

Put the covered casserole in the oven and microwave on medium until the meat is tender—about 10 minutes. Stir once during cooking. Pour the arrowroot and cider mixture into the casserole and microwave on high, stirring once during cooking, until the liquid thickens—about 5 minutes. Serve hot.

Golden Casserole

THIS NOURISHING DISH MAKES A COMPLETE MEAL
AND NEEDS NO ACCOMPANIMENT.

Serves 4

Working time: about 30 minutes

Total time: about 1 hour and 30 minutes

Calories 270, Protein 24g, Cholesterol 70mg, Total fat 8g,
Saturated fat 3g, Sodium 300mg

400 g/14 oz	*pork fillet, trimmed of fat and cut into 2.5 cm (1 inch) cubes*
1 tbsp	*safflower oil*
300 g/10 oz	*acorn, butternut or other winter squash*
400 g/14 oz	*sweet potatoes or eddoes, or a mixture of the two*
1/4 tsp	*saffron threads*
1/4 tsp	*crystal salt*
30 cl/1/2 pint	*unsalted vegetable stock*
1	*blade mace*
2	*whole allspice berries*
300 g/10 oz	*custard marrows, yellow courgettes or other summer squash*
100 g/31/2 oz	*baby sweetcorn*
1/4 tsp	*salt*

Preheat a browning dish for 5 to 7 minutes, or for the maximum time allowed in the manufacturer's instructions. Add the oil and the pork and stir vigorously for about 1 1/2 minutes until the meat is lightly browned. Transfer the meat to a casserole dish.

Pierce the skin of the acorn or butternut squash in two or three places with a skewer or sharp knife, then microwave it on high, on a double thickness of paper towels, for 5 minutes—it will now be softened and easy to cut. Peel and cut into 2.5 cm (1 inch) cubes.

Peel the sweet potatoes or eddoes, dice them into 2.5 cm (1 inch) cubes, and place them in the casserole dish with the meat. Using a mortar and pestle, grind the saffron with the crystal salt until pulverized. Warm the stock, dissolve the saffron and salt in it and pour the liquid into the casserole. Add the mace and allspice and microwave on high until the liquid begins to boil—about 5 minutes. Stir and cook for a further 15 minutes on medium low.

Remove the casserole from the microwave and add the acorn or butternut squash. Cook for a further 10 minutes on medium low.

Cut the custard marrows or courgettes into pieces slightly smaller than the rest of the vegetables and the meat. Wash the baby sweetcorn, keeping these whole if under 5 cm (2 inches) in length. Add the custard marrows or courgettes and sweetcorn to the casserole and cook for a final 10 minutes on medium low.

Remove the mace and allspice and add the salt. The golden liquid will be clear and thin. Serve hot.

EDITOR'S NOTE: In place of the fillet, you can substitute a more dense, muscular cut such as neck end or the fillet end of leg in this recipe. Trim the meat of all visible fat, and allow about 15 minutes longer cooking time before adding the custard marrow or courgettes and sweetcorn.

Kofta with Curry Sauce and Cucumber

COMMON IN INDIAN AND MIDDLE EASTERN COOKERY, KOFTA CONSISTS OF MINCED MEAT
WITH SEASONINGS SHAPED INTO BALLS OR SAUSAGE SHAPES.

Serves 8
Working (and total) time: about 55 minutes
Calories 230, Protein 22g, Cholesterol 65mg, Total fat 11g, Saturated fat 3g, Sodium 275mg

750 g/1¹/₂ lb	*trimmed leg or neck end of pork, minced*
¹/₄ tsp	*chilli powder*
1¹/₂ tsp	*ground turmeric*
1 tsp	*ground cardamom*
¹/₂ tsp	*salt*
1 cm/¹/₂ inch	*piece fresh ginger root, chopped*
2 tbsp	*besan flour or soya flour*
2 tsp	*finely chopped coriander leaves*
1 tsp	*finely chopped parsley prigs*
250 g/8 oz	*cucumber, sliced into 4 cm (1¹/₂ inch)*
	lengths and quartered

Curry sauce

2 tbsp	*safflower oil*
250 g/8 oz	*onions, very finely chopped*
1	*garlic clove, crushed*
2.5 cm/1 inch	*piece cinnamon stick*
4	*cloves*
2 tbsp	*ground coriander*
2 tbsp	*ground cumin*
¹/₄ tsp	*chilli powder*
1	*bay leaf*
¹/₂ tsp	*salt*
250 g/8 oz	*potatoes, grated*
500 g/1 lb	*ripe tomatoes, skinned and seeded, or*
	250 g canned whole tomatoes

To prepare the sauce, first preheat a large browning dish for 5 to 7 minutes, or for the maximum time allowed in the manufacturer's instructions. Add the oil and onion and microwave, uncovered, on high, stirring occasionally, until the onions are softened and slightly brown—about 5 minutes. Stir in the garlic, cinnamon stick, cloves, coriander, cumin, chilli powder, bay leaf and salt, and microwave on high for 30 seconds. Add the potatoes, tomatoes and 45 cl (³/₄ pint) of water; cover and cook on high for 20 minutes, stirring occasionally; if covering with plastic film, leave a corner open to allow steam to escape.

While the sauce is cooking, put the chilli powder, turmeric, cardamom, salt, ginger and flour into a bowl, add the chopped coriander and parsley, and mix together. Shape the mixture into 16 sausage shapes or balls and set them aside.

When the sauce ingredients have cooked, purée them in a food processor or blender, pass them through a sieve, then return the sauce to the dish. Arrange the kofta in the dish, cover and microwave on high for 5 minutes. Rearrange the kofta, exchanging those in the centre with the ones round the edges. Baste the kofta with the sauce and microwave on high for 2 minutes, then add the cucumber pieces and cook for 1 minute more.

EDITOR'S NOTE: Besan flour is made from ground chickpeas and lentils. Poppadoms may be cooked in the microwave oven on high until they are puffy—about 1 minute.

Stuffed Chops with Kidney Bean and Juniper Sauce

Serves 4

Working time: about 20 minutes

Total time: about 35 minutes

Calories 425, Protein 40g, Cholesterol 70mg, Total fat 15g, Saturated fat 5g, Sodium 110mg

4	*pork chops (about 125 to 150 g/4^1/$_2$ to 5 oz each), trimmed of fat*
30 g/1 oz	*pine-nuts*
60 g/2 oz	*cooked long-grain rice*
4	*fresh dates, stoned*
^{1}/$_2$ tsp	*dried rosemary*
1 tsp	*safflower oil*
Kidney bean and juniper sauce	
250 g/8 oz	*cooked kidney beans*
^{1}/$_4$ tsp	*freshly ground black pepper*
18	*juniper berries*
30 cl/^{1}/$_2$ pint	*unsalted vegetable stock*
2 tbsp	*tomato paste*

In a food processor, blend together the pine-nuts, rice, dates and rosemary. (Alternatively, chop the rice, dates and pine-nuts, and mix them by hand with the rosemary.) Cut a cavity in the side of each of the chops, and press the stuffing mixture into the cavities.

Preheat a browning dish for 5 to 7 minutes, or for the maximum time allowed in the manufacturer's instructions, and swirl the oil round the base of the dish. Pat the chops dry with paper towels to facilitate browning, and arrange them in the dish with the thickest part to the outside, pressing them down on to the browning surface with a spatula. When the sizzling stops, cook the chops on high for 1 minute before turning them over to brown the other side.

To make the sauce, purée the kidney beans, pepper, juniper berries, stock and tomato paste in a food processor or blender. Pour into a shallow dish and arrange the chops over the purée with the thicker part towards the outside of the dish.

Microwave on high, uncovered, until the chops are just cooked—about 7 minutes. Remove the chops from the dish and keep them warm.

Return the dish to the microwave and cook the sauce on high for 3 minutes to reduce and thicken it, stirring once during cooking. Pour the sauce on to the chops and serve immediately.

Celery Chops

Serves 4

Working time: about 15 minutes

Total time: about 40 minutes

Calories 200, Protein 25g, Cholesterol 70mg, Total fat 9g,
Saturated fat 4g, Sodium 390mg

4	boneless loin chops (about 125 g/4 oz each), trimmed of fat
350 g/12 oz	celery, cut into 2.5 cm (1 inch) pieces
15 cl/¼ pint	stout
15 cl/¼ pint	unsalted vegetable stock
½	onion, sliced
1 tsp	arrowroot, dissolved in 1 tbsp stout, stock or water
90 g/3 oz	smetana
1 to 2 tbsp	prepared English grainy mustard
1 tbsp	torn lovage leaves
1 tbsp	torn celery leaves
½ tsp	salt
	freshly ground black pepper

Place the celery in a dish with the stout, stock and onion. Bring to the boil on high, then cook on high for 10 to 15 minutes, or until tender.

Preheat a browning dish on high for 5 to 7 minutes, or for the maximum time allowed in the manufactur-er's instructions. Quickly arrange the chops in the dish with the thickest part to the outside and press down hard on to the browning surface with a spatula. Once the sizzling stops, cook the chops on high for 1 minute, then turn them over to brown the other side lightly.

Pour the celery and cooking liquid round the chops and cook on high for another minute, or until the liquid bubbles. Reduce the setting to medium and cook for 3 minutes, covered, giving the dish a quarter turn every minute. Allow to rest for 2 minutes, then test for doneness by cutting through the thickest part of a chop with the point of a sharp knife; if the meat is still pink, cook for 1 minute more and test as before. Repeat as necessary, but take care not to overcook. When fully cooked, drain the pork and celery, re-serving the cooking liquid, and keep warm while you make the sauce.

Beat the arrowroot mixture into the smetana, then add 1 tablespoon each of the mustard and reserved cooking liquid, stirring well. Cook on high for 1 to 2 minutes, until thickened, stirring every 20 seconds or so. Add the lovage and celery, the salt, some pepper, and the remaining mustard to taste. Pour the sauce over the pork and celery and serve immediately.

Chops with Aubergine Purée and Vegetables

Serves 4

Working (and total) time: about 45 minutes

Calories 250, Protein 26g, Cholesterol 70mg, Total fat 13g, Saturated fat 3g, Sodium 370mg

4	boned loin chops (about 125 g/4 oz each), trimmed of fat
500 g/1 lb	aubergines
1 tsp	safflower oil
90 g/3 oz	thick Greek yoghurt
1 tsp	salt
1/2 tsp	ground coriander
1/4 tsp	ground cumin
4	small fresh mint sprigs
	freshly ground black pepper
	Mediterranean vegetables
2	courgettes, sliced
1	sweet red pepper, seeded, deribbed and sliced
1	sweet yellow pepper, seeded, deribbed and sliced
1	tomato, sliced
1 tbsp	safflower oil
1/2	garlic clove, finely chopped
1 tbsp	finely chopped coriander

Pierce the skin of the aubergines in several places with the point of a sharp knife. Brush the skin with about 1/2 teaspoon of the oil, place the aubergines on a double thickness of absorbent paper towels and cook on high for 5 minutes, turning twice during this time.

The aubergines should be soft, but not collapsed,

and the skin fairly tender. When they are cool enough to handle, slice them into 2 cm (3/4 inch) thick rounds.

Preheat a browning dish on high for 5 to 7 minutes, or for the maximum time allowed in the manufacturer's instructions. Pat the chops dry with paper towels to facilitate browning and brush them with the remaining oil. When the browning dish is ready, quickly arrange the chops in it with the thickest part to the outside of the dish; press down hard with a spatula. Once the sizzling stops, cook the chops on high for 1 minute, then turn them over to lightly brown the other side.

Remove the chops and arrange the aubergine slices in the dish. Place the chops on top of the aubergines. Cover the dish with a lid or with greaseproof paper, and cook on medium for 5 minutes, giving the dish a quarter turn every minute. Allow to rest for 2 minutes, then test for doneness by cutting through the thickest part of a chop with the point of a sharp knife; if the meat is still pink, cook for 1 minute more on medium and test as before. Repeat the process as necessary, but take care not to overcook the chops. When fully cooked, remove the chops and keep them warm.

To prepare the vegetables, mix together the courgettes, sweet peppers and tomato with the safflower oil, garlic and chopped coriander. Microwave on high for 3 minutes.

To prepare the purée, blend or process together the aubergine, yoghurt, salt, ground coriander, cumin and mint. The purée should still be quite thick; if you wish, add any cooking juices which the aubergine did not absorb. Season with some black pepper and serve warm with the chops and vegetables.

Greek Casserole

Serves 4

Working time: about 15 minutes

Total time: about 1 hour

Calories 290, Protein 23g, Cholesterol 70mg, Total fat 8g,
Saturated fat 3g, Sodium 400 mg

400 g/14 oz	*lean roasting pork, cut into 2.5 cm (1 inch) cubes*
1 tbsp	*potato flour, seasoned with white pepper*
1 tsp	*virgin olive oil*
30 cl/¹/₂ pint	*unsalted veal or vegetable stock*
350 g/12 oz	*small (2.5 cm/1 inch) new potatoes, or larger potatoes cut into 2.5 cm (1 inch) cubes*
4	*dried pear halves*
2 tbsp	*chunky quince preserve*
2 tbsp	*honey, preferably Hymettus*
4	*fresh thyme sprigs*
¹/₂	*cinnamon stick*
2	*5 cm (2 inch) strips lemon rind*
1 tsp	*salt*
4 to 6 tbsp	*fresh lemon juice*
	freshly ground black pepper

Preheat a browning dish on high for 5 to 7 minutes, or for the maximum time allowed in the manufacturer's instructions. Toss the cubes of meat in the seasoned flour. Brush the browning dish with the oil and add the meat. Cook on high for 2 minutes, stirring frequently so that the meat browns evenly.

Heat the stock until it is almost boiling. Add 8 cl (3 fl oz) of the stock to the meat and cook for 2 minutes more on high, scraping the dish with a spatula to detach the brown sediment and thicken the sauce. Add the potatoes, pears, quince preserve, honey, thyme, cinnamon, lemon rind and retsina, and enough stock to cover the meat (which may otherwise discolour slightly). Continue to cook on high until the liquid comes to the boil—10 to 15 minutes. Stir the contents of the dish; cover and cook for another 30 to 45 minutes on medium low, until the meat is tender. Stir the contents of the dish once or twice during this time and add more stock if the liquid in the dish falls below the level of the meat.

Towards the end of the cooking time, add the salt and sufficient lemon juice to cut the sweetness pleasantly; a little more honey may be added if a sweeter taste is desired. Remove the cinnamon and thyme, season with some pepper and serve hot.

Picadillo

THIS ADAPTATION OF A LATIN AMERICAN FAVOURITE FEATURES SULTANAS, OLIVES AND CHICK-PEAS IN ADDITION TO THE CHOPPED MEAT.

Serves 6

Working time: about 45 minutes

Total time: about 3 hours (includes soaking)

Calories 225, Protein 18g, Cholesterol 35mg, Total fat 6g, Saturated fat 1g, Sodium 235mg

500 g/1 lb	*topside of beef, trimmed of fat and minced*
200 g/7 oz	*dried chick-peas, picked over*
1	*onion, chopped*
4	*garlic cloves, finely chopped*
1 tsp	*safflower oil*
800 g/1³/₄ lb	*canned whole tomatoes, drained and crushed*
75 g/2¹/₂ oz	*sultanas*
12	*green olives, stoned and rinsed*
¹/₂ tsp	*ground cinnamon*
¹/₂ tsp	*ground allspice*
¹/₄ tsp	*cayenne pepper*
2	*bay leaves*

Rinse the chick-peas under cold running water, then put them into a large, heavy saucepan with enough water to cover them by about 7.5 cm (3 inches).

Cover the pan, leaving the lid ajar, and slowly bring the liquid to the boil over medium-low heat. Boil the chick-peas for 2 minutes, then turn off the heat, and soak the chick-peas, covered, for at least 1 hour. Return the chick-peas to the boil, reduce the heat, and simmer them until they are tender—about 1 hour.

Combine the chopped onion, garlic and safflower oil in a large bowl, cover the bowl with plastic film and microwave the vegetables on high for 4 minutes. Add the minced beef and cook the mixture, uncovered, on medium (50 per cent power) for 5 minutes. Stir the beef, breaking it into small pieces, and cook it on medium for 3 minutes more.

Drain the chick-peas and add them to the beef mixture. Stir in the tomatoes, sultanas, olives, cinnamon, allspice, cayenne pepper and bay leaves. Cook the picadillo, uncovered, on high for 15 minutes, stirring every 5 minutes. Remove the bay leaves and let the picadillo stand for 5 minutes before serving.

EDITOR'S NOTE: Canned chick-peas can be used this recipe, thus greatly reducing the cooking time, but the sodium content of the dish will be increased.

Beef Braised on Mushrooms with Green Peppercorn Persillade

Serves 6

Working time: about 30 minutes

Total time: about 1 hour

Calories 200, Protein 25g, Cholesterol 60mg, Total fat 7g, Saturated fat 2g, Sodium 140mg

850 g/1¾ lb	*boned and rolled sirloin joint, trimmed of fat*
500 g/1 lb	*mushrooms, wiped clean and thinly sliced*
1	*onion, finely chopped*
1 tsp	*safflower oil*
2 tsp	*green peppercorns, rinsed*
30 g/1 oz	*parsley leaves*
3	*garlic cloves*
¼ tsp	*salt*
2 tbsp	*plain flour*

Combine the mushrooms, onion and oil in a 20 cm (8 inch) square baking dish. Cover the dish with plastic film and microwave the vegetables on high for 5 minutes.

While the mushrooms are cooking, prepare the green peppercorn persillade. Place the green peppercorns, parsley and garlic on a chopping board and sprinkle them with the salt; finely chop the mixture.

Pierce the roast in about 15 places with the tip of a small knife. Press some of the persillade into each of the incisions. Rub away any remaining persillade on the outside of the roast.

When the mushrooms have finished cooking, stir the flour into them. Set the roast on top of the mushrooms and cover the dish once again. Cook the meat on medium (50 per cent power) for 14 to 16 minutes for medium-rare meat. Let the roast stand, still covered, an additional 10 minutes before carving. (At this point, the internal temperature of the meat should have risen to 63°C (145°F); if it has not, microwave the roast on high for 2 to 3 minutes more.)

Cut the roast into very thin slices; divide the meat and mushrooms between six warmed dinner plates. Serve immediately.

53

Lime-Ginger Beef

Serves 4
Working time: about 25 minutes
Total time: about 45 minutes
Calories 240, Protein 25g, Cholesterol 65mg, Total fat 10g, Saturated fat 3g, Sodium 180mg

600 g/1¼ lb	rump steak, trimmed of fat and cut into thin strips
	freshly ground black pepper
1 tbsp	safflower oil
2	spring onions, trimmed and sliced into thin strips
1	large carrot, julienned
1	sweet red pepper, seeded, deribbed and julienned

Lime-ginger sauce

1	lime, grated rind and juice
1 tsp	grated fresh ginger root
2 tbsp	dry sherry
2 tsp	low-sodium soy sauce or shoyu
½ tsp	finely chopped garlic
1 tbsp	sugar
1 tbsp	cornflour, mixed with 4 tbsp water

Preheat a microwave browning dish on high for the maximum time allowed in the dish's instruction manual. While the dish is heating, combine all the ingredients for the lime-ginger sauce in a small bowl. Set the bowl aside. Season the beef strips with a generous grinding of black pepper.

When the browning dish is heated, brush ½ tablespoon of the oil evenly over the dish to coat it. Sear half of the beef strips on the dish, stirring and turning the meat with a wooden spoon. Once the beef has been seared—after 1 or 2 minutes—transfer it to a browning dish. Wipe off the browning dish with a paper towel and reheat it for 3 minutes. Brush the remaining oil on to the dish and sear the remaining beef in the same way. Add the beef to the baking dish.

Add the spring onions, carrot and red pepper to the beef. Pour the sauce over all and microwave the mixture on high for 3 minutes. Serve the beef and vegetables from the baking dish or transfer them to a platter; serve at once.

Meatballs in Caper Sauce

Serves 4 as an appetizer

Working time: about 20 minutes

Total time: about 30 minutes

Calories 120, Protein 14g, Cholesterol 35mg, Total fat 4g,
Saturated fat 1g, Sodium 190mg

300 g/10 oz	*topside of beef, trimmed of fat and minced*
1	*small onion, chopped*
1/4 litre/8 fl oz	*unsalted brown or chicken stock*
4 tbsp	*rolled oats*
1 tbsp	*chopped parsley*
1/4 tsp	*grated nutmeg lemon, grated rind only freshly ground black pepper*
1 tsp	*cornflour, mixed with 1 tbsp water*
1 tbsp	*plain low-fat yoghurt*
1 tsp	*soured cream*
1 tsp	*capers, rinsed and chopped*

Put the onion in a 1 litre (1³/₄ pint) baking dish. Cover the dish and microwave the onion on high for 3 min-utes. Transfer the onion to a bowl. Pour the stock into the baking dish and cook it on high until it comes to a simmer—about 4 minutes.

While the stock is heating, add the beef, rolled oats, ¹/₂ tablespoon of the parsley, the nutmeg, the lemon rind and a liberal grinding of pepper to the onion. Knead the mixture to mix it well, then form it into 16 meatballs. Drop the meatballs into the heated stock and cook them, covered, on high for 4 min-utes.

Using a slotted spoon, transfer the meatballs to a serving dish. Discard all but 12.5 cl (4 fl oz) of the cook-ing liquid in the baking dish; stir the cornflour mixture into this remaining liquid. Cook the liquid on high until it thickens—about 30 seconds. Turn off the heat and let the thickened stock cool for 1 minute, then stir in the yoghurt, soured cream, capers and the remaining parsley. Pour the sauce over the meatballs and serve them while they are still hot.

Chilli Meatballs
with Two Pepper Sauces

Serves 4

Working time: about 30 minutes

Total time: about 40 minutes

Calories 225, Protein 25g, Cholesterol 60mg, Total fat 8g,
Saturated fat 3g, Sodium 175mg

350 g/12 oz	*lean lamb (from the leg or loin), trimmed of fat and minced*
1	*stick celery, finely chopped*
60 g/2 oz	*fresh wholemeal breadcrumbs*
2	*small hot chilli peppers, finely chopped*
2 tbsp	*finely cut chives, plus a few chives for garnish*
1 tsp	*anchovy essence*
1/4 tsp	*salt*
1 tsp	*virgin olive oil*

Pepper sauces

1	*sweet red pepper*
1	*sweet yellow pepper*
2 tsp	*white wine vinegar*
2 tbsp	*thick Greek yoghurt*

First make the sauces. Prick the sweet peppers in several places with a fork or skewer, place them, spaced well apart, on a double layer of paper towels in the microwave oven and cook them on high until they are soft—about 5 minutes—turning them once. Place the peppers in a bowl, cover with plastic film, and leave for 5 to 10 minutes. Skin and seed the peppers. Roughly chop the red pepper and purée it in a blender or food processor with 1 teaspoon of the vinegar and 2 tablespoons of water until smooth. Transfer the purée to a small bowl and stir in 1 tablespoon of the yoghurt. Process the yellow pepper in the same way, transfer it to a separate bowl and stir in the remaining yoghurt.

To make the meatballs, mix together the lamb, celery, breadcrumbs, chillies, cut chives, anchovy essence and salt. Using your hands, form the mixture into 20 balls each about 2.5 cm (1 inch) in diameter.

Preheat a browning dish following the manufacturer's instructions. Immediately add the olive oil and meatballs, turning the meatballs until they stop sizzling. Cover them with a lid, or plastic film with a corner pulled back, and cook them on high for 5 minutes, turning once. Leave them to stand for 3 minutes.

Meanwhile, heat the sauces on medium for 1 1/2 minutes; if the bowls are small enough, they should fit in the oven together. Spoon the red pepper sauce round the edge of four warmed serving plates, and spoon the yellow pepper sauce into the centre. Use a skewer to draw a pattern in the sauces.

Distribute the meatballs among the plates. Serve them immediately, garnished with the chives.

Meat Loaf with Olives

Serves 6

Working time: about 15 minutes

Total time: about 30 minutes

Calories 275, Protein 32g, Cholesterol 85mg, Total fat 12g,
Saturated fat 5g, Sodium 320mg

850 g/1³/₄ lb	*lean lamb (from the leg or loin), trimmed of fat and minced*
1	*egg white, lightly beaten*
1 tbsp	*chopped fresh oregano, or 1 tsp dried oregano*
¹/₄ tsp	*cayenne pepper*
2	*garlic cloves, finely chopped*
4 tbsp	*finely chopped onion*
30 g/1 oz	*parsley, chopped*
6	*oil-cured black olives, stoned and finely chopped*
60 g/2 oz	*dry breadcrumbs*
4 tbsp	*freshly grated Parmesan cheese*
1 tbsp	*red wine vinegar*
1¹/₂ tbsp	*tomato paste*

In a large bowl, combine the egg white, oregano, cayenne pepper, garlic and onion. Add the lamb, parsley, olives, breadcrumbs, Parmesan cheese, vinegar and 1 tablespoon of the tomato paste. Using a wooden spoon, mix all the ingredients together until they are well combined.

Shape the meat mixture into a log about 7.5 cm (3 inches) in diameter. Place the log in a shallow baking dish and spread the remaining ¹/₂ tablespoon of tomato paste over the surface of the meat. Cook the loaf, uncovered, on high for 10 to 12 minutes, rotating the dish a half turn midway through the cooking time. Let the meat loaf stand for 10 minutes. To serve, cut the loaf into 12 slices.